SECRET HEROES OF WORLD WAR II

SECRET HEROES OF WORLD WAR II

TALES OF COURAGE FROM THE WORLDS OF ESPIONAGE AND RESISTANCE

ERIC CHALINE

METRO BOOKS
New York

METRO BOOKS
New York

An Imprint of Sterling Publishing Co., Inc.
1166 Avenue of the Americas
New York, NY 10036

ISBN 978-1-4351-6251-8

For information about custom editions, special sales, and
premium and corporate purchases, please contact
Sterling Special Sales at 800-805-5489
or specialsales@sterlingpublishing.com.

Manufactured in China

2 4 6 8 10 9 7 5 3 1

www.sterlingpublishing.com

Design and illustration by Tony Seddon
Cover design by Mike Lebihan

Conceived, designed, and produced by
Quid Publishing
Part of The Quarto Group
Level 4 Sheridan House
114 Western Road
Hove BN3 1DD
England

www.quidpublishing.com

To Attila, for his friendship, help, and support

Contents

Introduction

At the time of writing, we are in the midst of remembering the first conflict that engulfed our planet between 1914–18. In many respects, the "Great War" was a dress rehearsal for the even more tragic and destructive event that took place two decades later. While World War I was the first mechanized conflict, World War II was the first technological war, during which battles were won not just by men slugging it out on the battlefield in ships, aircraft, and tanks, but by scientists in secret research bunkers and laboratories.

As Germany began to lose the war, Hitler increasingly looked to the development of an arsenal of advanced secret weapons to reverse the tide of defeats, including the A-bomb and the V-1 and V-2 flying bombs. This prompted a technological response from the Allies. The new battlefields of the mind called for a new breed of warrior, whose weapons of choice were the design table, the equation, and the slide-rule. Section one, Backroom heroes, features men on the scientific frontline, including mathematician and codebreaker Alan Turing (pp. 32–35), nuclear scientists Enrico Fermi (pp. 12–15) and Julius Oppenheimer (pp. 28–31), and radar pioneer Robert Watson-Watt (pp. 36–39).

The Axis and Allied powers had been fighting a secret war long before the outbreak of hostilities in 1939. Espionage is as old as war itself, but during World War II both sides had access to technologies to transmit information in ways undreamed of in earlier conflicts. Instantaneous radio communications were the means by which Allied spymasters in London, Moscow, and Washington were able to manage their intelligence networks. Spies listened to one another's transmissions and used radio to disseminate not just instructions and propaganda but also misinformation and deception. World War II also saw many thousands of women serve as secret agents across occupied Europe.

LEFT:
The Allied response to Nazi Germany's declaration of "Total War" involved an army of scientists, engineers, and spies.

Section two, Espionage heroes, features double agents, such as Eddie Chapman (pp. 46–49) and Dušan Popov (pp. 80–83), SOE operatives, such as Christine Granville (pp. 54–57), Violette Szabo (pp. 98–101), and Noor-un-Nisa Inayat Khan (pp. 66–69), and Russian spymaster Richard Sorge (pp. 94–97).

World War I had been fought by kingdoms and empires little changed since the settlement of Europe reached at the Congress of Vienna in 1814–15. World War II was also fought over territorial claims and economic advantage, but another much more dangerous element was added to the mix: ideology. The fascist powers Germany and Italy, allied to militaristic Japan, fought Soviet Russia and liberal-democratic England, France, and the United States. Nazi ideology, however, went far beyond defining a social, economic, and political system; it used eugenic pseudoscience to justify the enslavement and elimination of all "inferior" (ie, "non-German") peoples, and the murder of all those considered "unworthy" to live in the 1,000-year Reich, such as members of the LGBT community and the physically and mentally disabled.

Sections three and four, Resistance and Escape heroes, feature men and women who resisted and fought against the evils of fascism and militarism in Japan, Germany, and occupied Europe, either by direct action against German forces, by escaping from captivity in order to return to the fight, or by engineering the escape of persecuted minorities. They include Claus von Stauffenberg (pp. 168–171), Andrée Borrel (pp. 128–131), Jean Moulin (pp. 148–151), Pierre Brossolette (pp. 132–135), Dietrich Bonhoeffer (pp. 124–127), Douglas Bader (pp. 176–179), and Oskar Schindler (pp. 204–207).

Backroom heroes

We think of war as a quintessentially human pursuit sustained by the courage and fortitude of soldiers, sailors, and airmen, and the leadership, vision, and strategic genius of generals, and we can easily forget the importance of science, technology, and engineering in its conduct and outcome. If World War I was the first mechanized war that saw the introduction of tanks and aircraft into what had for centuries been the preserve of the infantry, cavalry, and artillery, World War II was the first technological war. The second world conflict was not only fought by men and their weapons on bloody battlefields across the globe, but also in secret laboratories, by scientists and engineers working in computing, cryptography, physics, chemistry, medicine, and avionics, who fought just as hard to give their side the technological edge over the enemy.

NAME: **Enrico Fermi**

NATIONALITY: Italian

BIRTH: September 29, 1901

DEATH: November 28, 1954

PROFESSION: Experimental and theoretical physicist

CATEGORY: Backroom hero

ACHIEVEMENT: He built the world's first nuclear reactor, proving the feasibility of nuclear weapons.

Imagine a world in which Hitler and Mussolini had won World War II. This nightmare scenario was only avoided because Enrico Fermi and many other brilliant German and Italian physicists opposed to fascism and anti-Semitism emigrated to England and the USA rather than give the Nazis the secrets of the A-bomb.

It is one of the great ironies of history and the greatest stroke of good fortune for the Allies that, although much of the early theoretical work that led to the successful development of the first atomic bombs in 1945 was done by German and Italian scientists, many of them preferred to defect to England and the USA rather than work for the Axis powers. Brilliant physicists, such as Albert Einstein (1879–1955), who were Jewish, or Enrico Fermi, whose wife was Jewish, emigrated rather than face an uncertain future in their homelands. Had it not been for the anti-Semitic atrocities of the Nazis and their allies, Italy's *Fascisti*, Hitler could have had the A-bomb before the USA, with disastrous consequences for the Allied war effort and the future history of humanity: Imagine an Axis victory or a nuclear standoff between the USA and the Third Reich.

Enrico Fermi was a brilliant Italian theoretical and experimental physicist, who, at the age of 24, was appointed to the newly created chair of physics at Sapienza University, Rome. In 1933, he postulated the existence of a new subatomic particle, the neutrino, which was a product of nuclear decay. This key discovery in nuclear physics won him the Nobel Prize in 1938. Yet, despite his many scientific achievements, Fermi felt unable to remain in Italy and work for Mussolini's fascist dictatorship. In 1928 he had married antifascist activist and writer, Laura Capon, and in 1938, when Mussolini enacted new racial laws to bring Italy into line with the anti-Semitic policies of Nazi Germany, Fermi decided not return to Rome after he had collected his Nobel Prize in Stockholm, but instead escaped with his wife and two children to New York.

BELOW:
Looking more like a pile of junk than a scientific experiment, the homespun Chicago Pile-1 was the first step in the creation of viable nuclear weapons.

ABOVE:

The X-10 Graphite reactor at Oak Ridge, Tennessee, was the world's second nuclear reactor; it began producing plutonium for the Manhattan Project in 1943.

Fermi's mistake

In 1923, when reviewing Einstein's famous equation, $e = mc^2$, Fermi wrote: "It does not seem possible, at least in the near future, to find a way to release these dreadful amounts of energy—which is all to the good because the first effect of an explosion of such a dreadful amount of energy would be to smash into smithereens the physicist who had the misfortune to find a way to do it." He would prove himself conclusively wrong within two decades, but he was not in bad company. In 1932, Einstein himself dismissed the idea of harnessing the power of the atom, saying, "There is not the slightest indication that nuclear energy will ever be obtainable."

When Fermi learned of the latest breakthroughs German scientists had made in the field of atomic fission—the basis for nuclear weapons—he quickly revised his opinion. He fully endorsed the contents of a letter, sent by Einstein and American-Hungarian physicist Leo Szilárd to President Roosevelt (1882–1945) in 1939, warning him that the Germans might develop the A-bomb first. The letter persuaded the U.S. government that everything necessary must be done to win the nuclear arms race. In 1942, the various committees and research bureaus set up to initiate the process were brought together in the Manhattan Project (1942–46; see Robert Oppenheimer, pp. 28–31). Invited to take part in the project, Fermi immediately started to work on plans for an experimental nuclear pile— the prototype for the nuclear reactors that would produce enriched fissile material for the first A-bombs. The timing was critical, as the Allies had no idea how far the Germans had got with their own research.

The road to Trinity

Fermi's team was assigned the task of designing and building a reactor that could produce fissile uranium-235 and plutonium-239. The result was the world's first nuclear reactor, the Chicago Pile-1 (see Feature, right), which succeeded in creating the first self-sustained manmade nuclear chain reaction. The achievement prompted a coded telephone message from Fermi's boss on the Manhattan Project, physicist Arthur Compton (1892–1962), to the chair of the National Defense Research Committee: "You'll be interested to know that the Italian navigator has just landed in the New World. The Earth was not as large as he had estimated, and he arrived at the New World sooner than he had expected." Although they did not know it at the time, Compton and Fermi had just ensured Allied victory over Japan in 1945.

Fermi tested and refined his reactor, taking part in the construction of the X-10 Graphite Reactor at Oak Ridge, Tennessee, in 1943, and of the much larger water-cooled B Reactor at the Hanford Site, Washington State, the following year. In mid-1944 he became associate head of the laboratory in Los Alamos, New Mexico, which was developing two experimental nuclear devices: "Little Boy," a uranium-235 bomb, thought to be the most reliable design, but which was never tested because of a shortage of fissile uranium; and the "Fat Man," a more complex plutonium-239 bomb, which was detonated at the Trinity Test in New Mexico on July 16, 1945. Fermi agreed that the bombs should be dropped on industrial targets in Japan without prior warning. Little Boy destroyed Hiroshima on August 6 and Fat Man, Nagasaki, three days later. Japan surrendered on August 15, ending the war in the Asia-Pacific region and saving an estimated 1 million Allied lives.

FEATURE **Junk pile**

The unlikely location of the world's first nuclear reactor was a racket sports court beneath the west stand of Stagg Field, a disused football stadium owned by the University of Chicago. The homespun reactor was a pile of uranium and graphite blocks held together by a brick and timber armature. The theory held that nuclear fission would begin when free neutrons released by the natural decay of uranium atoms were absorbed by other uranium atoms. The graphite blocks packed around the uranium acted as a neutron moderator, slowing the particles down, thereby increasing the chance that they would be absorbed. The control rods designed to dampen the reaction were made of neutron-absorbing cadmium, indium, and silver. Unlike later reactors, Chicago Pile-1 had no cooling system and no radiation shielding. Nevertheless, on December 2, 1942, the pile went critical, triggering the world's first manmade self-sustaining fission reaction.

Howard Florey

NAME: **Howard Florey**

NATIONALITY: Australian

BIRTH: September 24, 1898

DEATH: February 21, 1968

PROFESSION: Doctor, pharmacologist, and pathologist

CATEGORY: Backroom hero

ACHIEVEMENT: He transformed an accidental discovery into an effective drug that saved countless millions.

It is well known that Sir Alexander Fleming discovered the world's first antibiotic, penicillin, after leaving a petri dish out over the summer. History, however, has been less generous in recording the contributions of other researchers, such as Dr. Howard Florey, who turned a scientific curiosity into a workable treatment for the most common infectious diseases.

The previous entry considered the disastrous outcome had Germany obtained the A-bomb before the Allies. This entry poses a "what if" scenario of even more horrifying import for humanity: What if antibiotics had never been discovered or successfully developed? For one thing there would be far fewer of us alive today, and the quality of our lives would be far worse, because minor injuries and common infectious diseases could easily turn into life-threatening conditions. The prewar situation was described by a doctor in the following terms: "Every hospital had a septic ward, filled with patients with chronic discharging abscesses, sinuses, septic joints, and sometimes meningitis." It is a medical horror story that our children and grandchildren may have to face as the number of antibiotic-resistant strains of bacteria continues to increase.

Such was the state of the world before 1940, when an insignificant scratch could lead to a fatal infection (see Feature, p. 19). There is now some doubt as to exactly how the discovery that some *Penicillium* fungi could kill disease-causing bacteria came about. The myth is that Fleming, who was famously untidy, left a petri dish of *Staphylococcus* bacteria uncovered just before he went on holiday in summer, 1928. When he returned, he found no bacteria where the mold had grown on the dish. The *Penicillium* would have made its way onto the dish by chance, but a more logical explanation is that the mold was a contaminant from a culture in a lab one floor below.

What is not in doubt, however, is that Fleming, who was a typical nerd and not a gifted communicator, failed to disseminate the importance of his discovery, thereby delaying the development of effective antibiotics by a decade. There were small-scale trials of penicillin during the 1930s, but with varying results. It was only in 1940, after a team working at the Sir William Dunn School of Pathology in Oxford, which included Ernst Chain (1906–79) and Howard Florey, had subjected penicillin to a rigorous process of testing to evaluate its effects *in vitro* (ie, outside of a typical biological host) and in infected mice, that the full impact of the compound was fully appreciated.

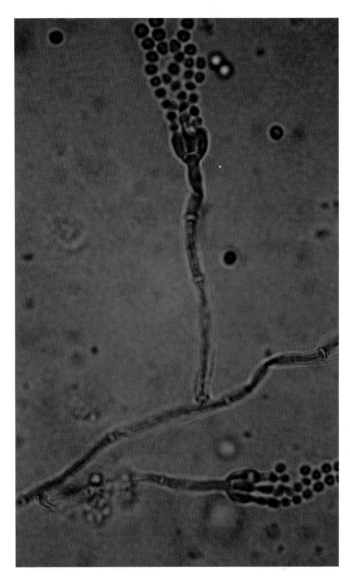

ABOVE:
After *Penicillium* mold infected samples he had left uncovered in his lab, Fleming realized that something in the mold could kill disease-causing bacteria.

ABOVE:

Fleming first saw the effect of *Penicillium* mold on bacteria, but it was a team led by Florey that developed his discovery into the first antibiotic compound.

"It looks like a miracle."

These were the words with which Florey greeted the first trials of penicillin in mice. Sepsis, an inflammatory response to infection that can now be cured with a few tablets, was the Ebola of its day, difficult to treat and often fatal. The realization of his own powerlessness led a newly qualified Dr. Howard Florey to say that the worst part of being a doctor was "the appalling thing of seeing young people maimed or wiped out while one can do nothing." And this was in peacetime Australia. Imagine how much worse conditions were in times of war, when injured men succumbed in their thousands to wounds, both major and minor, that went septic, and the only hope to save a man's life, if the infection was in one of his limbs, was amputation.

The year 1940 was the *annus horribilis* for the Allied cause. In May, France fell to Hitler's *Blitzkrieg* and English troops were evacuated from Dunkirk. In Europe the Axis advance seemed unstoppable. But in an Oxford laboratory that year, a quite different kind of victory was being won: Florey cured infected mice with penicillin. Although he did realize that he was involved in something that would change the world, Florey remained strangely detached. Speaking later about his breakthrough, he said:

> *People sometimes think that I and the others worked on penicillin because we were interested in suffering humanity. I don't think it ever crossed our minds about suffering humanity. This was an interesting scientific exercise, and because it was of some use in medicine is very gratifying, but this was not the reason that we started working on it.*

But in this case, perhaps what was needed was a hardheaded, practical doctor, such as Florey, rather than an absent-minded scientist, such as

Fleming may occasionally have been. Florey described himself as an "academic highway robber," who went after every grant to keep his research going. In 1941 Florey was ready to go to the USA to discuss production of the new drug with U.S. pharmaceutical companies. Initially, progress was frustratingly slow.

In March 1942, half the total penicillin produced in the USA was used in treating one patient suffering from streptococcal septicemia. By June, there was enough to treat ten more. With the country now fully engaged in the European and Pacific theaters, the War Production Board stepped in with plans to make the drug available to all Allied troops fighting in Europe. As the Allies landed on the Normandy beaches in spring, 1944, they could count on 2.3 million doses of American-produced penicillin. By the closing days of the war, production had increased to 646 billion units annually. Florey's war against disease was the antithesis of events on the battlefield: he fought to preserve human life, not to take it.

BELOW:
The introduction of antibiotics dramatically reduced the incidence of fatal cases of sepsis caused by common bacteria such as *Streptococcus* and *Staphylococcus*.

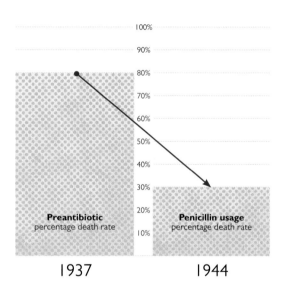

Preantibiotic percentage death rate
1937

Penicillin usage percentage death rate
1944

FEATURE · **Patient Zero**

You would not think twice, if you got a scratch from a rose thorn in the garden. And when this happened to 44-year-old Constable Albert Alexander of the Oxford police in December 1940, he did not either. One month later, however, he was rushed to the hospital with serious *Staphylococcus* and *Streptococcus* infections. When the case was brought to Florey's attention, he found a patient who was so close to death that he could become the first recipient of experimental penicillin. On February 12, 1941, Alexander was injected with an intravenous infusion of 160 mg (200 units) of penicillin and immediately showed sign of recovery, proving the effectiveness and safety of the drug. Unfortunately, by the fifth day of treatment, the meager store of penicillin had run out, and no more could be made in time to save the patient. Alexander died on March 15, 1941.

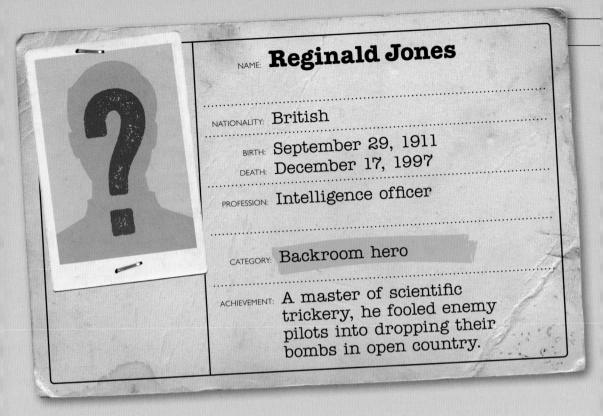

NAME: **Reginald Jones**

NATIONALITY: British

BIRTH: September 29, 1911
DEATH: December 17, 1997

PROFESSION: Intelligence officer

CATEGORY: Backroom hero

ACHIEVEMENT: A master of scientific trickery, he fooled enemy pilots into dropping their bombs in open country.

During World War I, pilots flew blind but had the element of surprise on their side. During World War II, developments in radio navigation guided German bombers to their targets with unprecedented accuracy. It was up to Reginald Jones to discover their secrets and then devise means of spoiling the *Luftwaffe's* party.

As we shall see in the next section, which deals with the heroes of wartime espionage, radio communication, through the broadcasts of the BBC and the radio transmitters that were dropped over occupied Europe, played a key role in the conduct of the war, disseminating information and misinformation. But radio waves played other militarily significant roles, because they could be used to guide bombers to their targets. The terror-bombing campaign against British cities, known as the Blitz (September 1940–May 1941), which Hitler hoped would force Britain out of the war, was fought both with aircraft and with invisible radio beams that raked the skies and deflected raids more effectively than any number of anti-aircraft batteries and interceptor fighters.

Not your average scientist

A new kind of war requires a new kind of warrior. Reginald Jones came
from a military family, but instead of taking the usual route for a career
in the army—officer training at Royal Military Academy Sandhurst, before
joining a regiment—he decided to study physics at Oxford University,
where he graduated with a First-class degree and then obtained his PhD.
The deeply patriotic Jones joined the Air Ministry as a scientific officer in
1936, convinced that his talents would be best employed combating what he
saw as the serious threat of Hitler's secret research establishments. In 1939,
as German tanks moved through Poland, Jones was on attachment to the
Admiralty (Navy Department). He returned to the Air Ministry as principal
scientific officer, with the official title of Assistant Director of Intelligence
(Science) in 1941, a post that he held for the remainder of the war.

Jones was not cast in the mold of the typical nerd. He was a tall, broad-
shouldered man who was not easily silenced. He would seldem relent when
debating his more conservative opponents in the armed forces, who would
occasionally oppose his proposals on grounds of cost or feasibility. He won
the confidence of the Chief of the Air Staff, Sir Charles Portal (1893–1971),
and of Prime Minister Winston Churchill (1874–1965), whom he briefed
on several occasions on German aircraft guidance systems, as well as the
secret weapons, such as the V-1 and V-2 flying
bombs, which an
increasingly desperate
Hitler deployed
against English cities
from continental
Europe in the
closing years
of the war.

BELOW:
Bombing raids started
before WWI, but
developments in aircraft
range, payload, and radio
guidance meant that by
WWII they were much
more destructive.

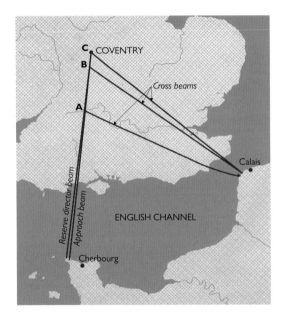

The Battle of the Beams

Jones' greatest contribution to the Allied war effort was his role in winning the "Battle of the Beams"—a high-stakes game of espionage, scientific advances, deception, and counter-deception played out during the German bombing campaign against British cities. The *Luftwaffe* had converted the civilian Lorenz radio navigation system, used to guide planes safely down to landing strips at night and in bad weather, into the military *Knickebein* ("crooked leg") system, which broadcast two radio beams from coastal stations that intersected over the desired target. One beam guided the plane toward the target and the second told the crew when to drop its payload.

Jones discovered how the system worked by piecing together information from Enigma decrypts (see Alan Turing, pp. 32–35) and the analysis of the *Knickebein* apparatus from a downed German bomber. Jones codenamed the German system "Headache," and with typical British humor christened his countermeasures "Aspirin." His first tactic was to jam the German signal, but then he discovered that by broadcasting a false signal on the same frequency, he could distort the beams, making the German aircrew think they were over their targets, when, in fact, they were dropping their bombs on open country.

TOP:
A Würzburg antenna
ABOVE:
In the X-Gerät system, three cross beams (A, B, and C) led bomber crews with greater accuracy to their target.

The Germans then deployed a more sophisticated guidance system called *X-Gerät* ("X-Apparatus"), which used four beams at a much higher frequency to guide their bombers. Although Jones was again able to analyze the system and devise effective countermeasures, these did not come in time to save the city of Coventry, whose center was destroyed on November 14,

---

FEATURE **The Oslo connection**

One of the most extraordinary pieces of intelligence handed to Reginald Jones was the Oslo Report, which outlined many of Germany's top-secret military programs. Written by German physicist Hans Meyer (1895–1980), the report was delivered to the British Embassy in the Norwegian capital and then sent to Jones to see if it was genuine. Along with details of new bombers, aircraft carriers, torpedoes, and electric fuses for ordnance, it also described remote-controlled gliders and rockets that the Germans would develop into the V-1 and V-2 flying bombs. But most useful of all for Jones were the detailed specifications of Germany's early warning radar and of the *Y-Gerät* range-finder system, which allowed him to develop effective countermeasures, saving the lives of countless British civilians and aircrew.

1940. When the Germans switched to the single-beam range-finder *Y-Gerät*, Jones again used Enigma decrypts and information passed to him in the Oslo Report (see Feature, above) to anticipate its deployment, and he was able to use countermeasures against the system as soon as it became operational. No further German radio guidance systems were deployed, as Hitler abandoned his plan to invade Britain and turned his attention eastward, launching the ill-fated invasion of Russia (Operation Barbarossa, 1941).

Radar war

Having won the Battle of the Beams, Churchill next tasked Jones with facilitating his plan for a sustained bombing campaign against Germany's cities and industrial regions. The Germans had developed their own early warning radar system, codenamed "Würzburg." Jones used reconnaissance photographs to locate Würzburg antennae, identifiable by their distinctive paraboloid form. Once indentified, Bomber Command were instructed to destroy them. In February 1942, using information provided by Gilbert Renault's (pp. 158–161) intelligence network, a raid was conducted against an isolated Würzburg station on the French Atlantic coast, which succeeded in capturing the main parts of the system and its operators (see Feature, p. 161).

As early as 1937, Jones had advocated dropping strips of paper coated with aluminum foil from aircraft before a night raid, as they would create thousands of false aircraft on the enemy's radar screens. Codenamed "Window," Jones' metallic chaff was deployed during a raid on Hamburg in July 1943, reportedly saving as many as 80 British bombers.

Although Reginald Mitchell made one of the most significant contributions to winning the Battle of Britain in 1940, he did not live to see the fighter plane he had designed, the Supermarine Spitfire, take on and defeat the mighty German *Luftwaffe*, or its role in the subsequent Allied victories in the European and Asia-Pacific theaters.

There can be few civilian inventions that have been militarized as quickly as the fixed-wing airplane. Only eight years after the Wright brothers had achieved the first flights in a powered, heavier-than-air aircraft in 1903, military airplanes had been deployed in a conflict between the Kingdom of Italy and the Ottoman Empire (1911–12). The first night bombing raid took place during the First Balkan War one year later, which pitted Greece and other Balkan states against the beleaguered Ottomans. Although the first long-range bombers were developed during World War I, the role of fixed-wing aircraft was limited in the main to reconnaissance flights and dogfights, and they possessed limited range, speed, and armaments. When the Germans bombed English cities, they used Zeppelin airships, the only aircraft of the day that could

carry a sufficient payload of bombs all the
way from the Continent to Britain.

The "Roaring Twenties" that followed World
War I were not just about noisy parties,
during which a lost generation tried to forget
the horrors of the Great War. They also
resonated to the roars of powerful engines.
This was the era of great air races that drew
millions of spectators, when aircraft
manufacturers from the leading industrial
powers, with the financial backing of their

governments and the support of their air forces, vied with one another to
produced ever-faster and more powerful aircraft. These peacetime contests
pitted past allies and future enemies against one another.

ABOVE:
The S-series assured
Supermarine's victory in
the Schneider trophy and
established Mitchell as the
leading aircraft designer
of his day.

King of the waves

Although Reginald Mitchell is best remembered today for his design of the
iconic World War II Supermarine Spitfire, it was one of the few aircraft
among the 24 he designed during his 20-year career that wasn't a seaplane.
Mitchell's forte was flying boats, and his true passion was racing floatplanes
that manufacturer Supermarine Aviation Works, based in Southampton,
UK, entered into the prestigious *Coupe Schneider* (Schneider Trophy), held
annually from 1913 to 1926 and then biannually until Supermarine won it
outright in 1931 (see Feature, p. 27).

Mitchell joined Supermarine in 1917, aged 22, becoming chief designer in
1919, chief engineer one year later, and technical director in 1927. He
established a good working relationship with the RAF, providing them with
a number of seaplanes, including the Sea Eagle, Scarab, Swan, and Stranraer.
He was considered so important to the firm that when Vickers bought
Supermarine, it was a condition of the sale that Mitchell would stay on as
head designer for five years. The sleek lines of Mitchell's S-series floatplanes
foreshadowed the distinctive profile of the Spitfire, which made it instantly
recognizable to friend and foe alike during the Battle of Britain and helped
establish its reputation.

A posthumous victory

Reginald Mitchell is unique in the annals of World War II in that he made a significant contribution to the Allied victory but he did not live to see his plane's "finest hour," dying of cancer two years before the outbreak of hostilities. Although the name Spitfire is now synonymous with the achievements of the wartime RAF, Mitchell himself did not like the name, which means someone with a fiery temper. When told the name Vickers and the RAF had come up with, he commented that it was "just the sort of bloody silly name they would choose."

The Spitfire was not the only fighter aircraft that fought during the Battle of Britain. When the number of enemy kills are added up, about 55 percent were accounted for by the Hawker Hurricane, the RAF's workhorse fighter to the Spitfire's thoroughbred. Nevertheless, it was the Spitfire that made the difference in the skies over Britain in 1940 and 1941. When the head of the *Luftwaffe*, Hermann Göring (1893–1946), asked German ace Adolf Galland (1912–96) what he needed to defeat the RAF, the pilot replied: "Spitfires."

BELOW:
The unforgettable lines of a thoroughbred. Although Hurricanes accounted for more enemy kills, it is the Spitfire that everyone associates with the Battle of Britain.

Birth of a legend

Mitchell's first attempt at designing a land-based fighter, the Supermarine Type 224, was a failure. The plane did not meet the specifications set by the RAF, which turned the design down in 1934. But with the blessing of his employers, Mitchell had already begun work on a more advanced design in 1933, which corrected the many shortcomings of the Type 224. He enclosed the cockpit, providing the pilot with oxygen-breathing apparatus, reduced drag with a retractable undercarriage, incorporated the new, more powerful Rolls-Royce Merlin engine, and swapped the thick "gull-wings" for a much thinner, lighter elliptical design.

Beverley Shenstone, his aerodynamicist, explained his choice of wing shape: "The ellipse was simply the shape that allowed us the thinnest possible wing with room inside to carry the necessary structure and the things we wanted to cram in. And it looked nice." The prototype's performance was so impressive that even before it had completed its trials, the RAF had ordered 310 of the still unnamed aircraft.

BELOW:
Thanks to his success with the S-series floatplanes, Mitchell won the confidence of the RAF, which commissioned him to design their new fighter.

FEATURE **Three times a winner**

The Schneider Trophy (1913–31) was typical of the many contests held during the interwar years that encouraged technical advances in aircraft design and performance. The race was a time trial for floatplanes held on a 217-mile (350km) triangular course. Mitchell's first entry for the race was a biplane, the Sea Lion II, which triumphed in Naples with an average speed of 145.72 mph (234km/h). In 1924, Mitchell's S.4 was unable to compete because it was damaged before the race. Supermarine returned to the cup in 1927, with government backing and the loan of crack RAF pilots. The S.5 placed first and second, with an average speed of 281.66 mph (453.28km/h). Mitchell won again with the S.6 in 1929, with an average speed of 238.64 mph (528.89km/h). His third victory in a row in 1931 with the S.6B, which averaged 340.08 mph (547.31km/h), brought the biannual competition to an end.

NAME:	**Robert Oppenheimer**
NATIONALITY:	American
BIRTH:	April 22, 1904
DEATH:	February 18, 1967
PROFESSION:	Theoretical physicist
CATEGORY:	Backroom hero
ACHIEVEMENT:	He directed the team of scientists that developed, built, and tested the first atomic bombs.

The man who directed the Manhattan Project's secret weapons laboratory at Los Alamos was perhaps not the most obviously suitable candidate, given that he was a socially inept, difficult man with leftwing sympathies. Yet his military superiors saw in him the drive and ambition that were needed to bring the project to a successful conclusion.

If you were looking for a man to direct the development, manufacture, and testing of the most destructive and terrifying weapons that humanity has ever created, would you choose a brilliant, well-balanced Nobel laureate who was good with people and had a firm grip on reality? Or would you choose a character in the mold of Sheldon Cooper from the TV series *The Big Bang Theory*? This was the choice faced by Lieutenant General

Leslie Groves (1896–1970) who, in 1942, was tasked with finding a man to oversee the Manhattan Project's secret weapons laboratory at Los Alamos, New Mexico, which would build the first atomic weapons (see Feature, p. 30).

Without wishing to be unkind to Robert Oppenheimer, anyone reading his biography will be struck by his resemblance to the dysfunctional,

geeky physicist in Lorre and Prady's hit sitcom *The Big Bang Theory*.
General Groves, however, found in him not just the breadth of knowledge
that was needed to successfully manage the most brilliant scientists of his
generation in the most complex scientific project ever attempted, but also an
"overweening ambition" that he thought would ensure the project's success.
It was an astute gamble, one that, according to physicist and Manhattan
consultant Isidor Rabi (1898–1988), was "a real stroke of genius" on the
part of a man "who was not generally considered to be a genius."

An unlikely leader

The son of German-Jewish immigrants, Oppenheimer was a gifted school
and college student, graduating *summa cum laude* from Harvard. But though
he might have excelled in abstract reasoning and scholarship, he was an
indifferent laboratory technician. Oppenheimer failed to impress at Oxford
and Cambridge, and he was on such poor terms with his Cambridge
professor that he once left a poisoned apple on his desk. He left England
and went to Germany to study for his doctorate under the supervision of
theoretical physicist, and father of quantum mechanics, Max Born (1882–
1970). After Oppenheimer's oral defense of his thesis, one of his examiners
said, relieved, "I'm glad that's over. He was on the point of questioning *me*."

ABOVE:

"Jumbo"—a massive steel container designed to preserve the meager stocks of plutonium should the Trinity Test end in whimper rather than a massive bang.

To his friends and students, Oppenheimer was both brilliant and charming, but for many of his acquaintances and colleagues, he was hard to get to know and even harder to like. He was a tall, emaciated chain smoker, who was so overbearing in seminars that his fellow students complained to Born about him. Yet there was also something very compelling about him. On his return to the USA both Caltech and Harvard offered him fellowships and had to agree to share him for a year. He was easily drawn to the company of women, including the wife of his friend and colleague, chemist Linus Pauling (1901–94). Pauling broke off relations with him as a result. Oppenheimer married but continued to see his old girlfriends.

If his character and unconventional personal life were not cause enough for the military to be wary of appointing him to the war's most sensitive scientific post, he also had strong leftwing views, which he did not even bother to hide. He joked on a 1942 security questionnaire that he'd been "a member of just about every Communist Front organization on the West Coast." But despite efforts to have him sacked for suspicious behavior in 1943, Groves was adamant that Oppenheimer should remain, declaring: "He is absolutely essential to the project."

FEATURE **The road to Manhattan**

The development of the A-bomb, from contested hypothesis to successfully detonated device in five years, is a particularly impressive achievement, given that it was accomplished during wartime and by nations whose economies were already stretched to breaking point. Their will to succeed underlines the very real fear of a Nazi nuclear apocalypse, had Hitler obtained the bomb first. Beginning modestly in 1939 on various university campuses and in military research establishments across the USA, UK, and Canada, the Manhattan Project grew into a global research and development (R&D) behemoth, controlled from Los Alamos, New Mexico, by General Groves and Julius Oppenheimer. Even by the standards of the present day, Manhattan was "big science"—it had a budget of $2 billion ($27 billion in 2015) and a staff of 130,000, working across more than 30 sites.

Down New Mexico way

When General Groves was looking for a secret location, where all the project's scientific personnel could gather to work on the design and assembly of the bombs, it was on Oppenheimer's recommendation that he chose Los Alamos, New Mexico. Oppenheimer had a particular affinity for the area, where he had leased a ranch, which he'd called *Perro Caliente* ("hot dog"), after his exclamation upon seeing it for the first time. He later said that physics and the desert were his "two great loves." He suggested the nearby Los Alamos Ranch School, near Santa Fe, which fit the Army's criteria of being 200 miles (320km) from anywhere and west of the Mississippi.

Unlike Enrico Fermi (see pp. 12–15), or the many other Nobel laureates who worked under him at Los Alamos, Oppenheimer was not a gifted experimental physicist. He was the scientific administrator of a facility that would grow to employ thousands, and the linkman that smoothed relations between the project's scientists and the military—men and women whose cultures could not have been more different. According to theoretical physicist Victor Weisskopf (1908–2002), his contribution did not come in the shape of ideas: "It was his continuous and intense presence, which produced a sense of direct participation in all of us; it created that unique atmosphere of enthusiasm and challenge that pervaded the place throughout its time."

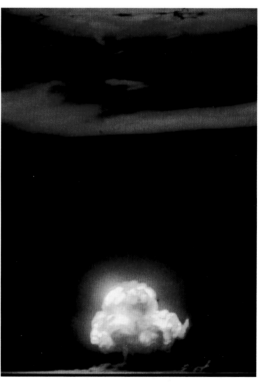

BELOW:
Oppenheimer's triumphant "It worked!" welcomed the Trinity Test that confirmed the viability of the nuclear weapons before they were deployed over Japan in August 1945.

Groves had read Oppenheimer perfectly and understood his overriding need to succeed in the task that had been set him. After the Trinity Test, Oppenheimer exclaimed gleefully, "It worked!" At an assembly at Los Alamos on the day of the atomic bombing of Hiroshima, he took to the stage and clasped his hands together over his head like a victorious prizefighter basking in the adulation of his fans.

NAME: **Alan Turing**

NATIONALITY: British

BIRTH: June 23, 1912
DEATH: June 7, 1954

PROFESSION: Mathematician

CATEGORY: Backroom hero

ACHIEVEMENT: The man who cracked German Enigma encryption, saving thousands of lives and changing the course of the war.

While still in his twenties, the soft-spoken Cambridge mathematician was the presiding genius of Bletchley Park, Britain's most secret intelligence center during World War II. He was the prime mover in the cracking of Germany's supposedly unbreakable Enigma code, which allowed the Allies to anticipate Hitler's every move.

By any reckoning, Alan Turing is one of the most remarkable scientists and mathematicians that Britain has ever produced. His wartime achievements, which were shrouded in secrecy not only at the time but for many years afterward, were prodigious. But much more significant was his conception of the "Universal Turing Machine" (UTM), which he outlined in a paper that predated the outbreak of war by four years.

Immediately after the war, Turing began working on turning what had up until then been a theoretical proposition into the Automatic Computing Engine, the first UTM and the forerunner of all modern-day computers.

Turing summed up what this meant in 1948: "We do not have to have an infinity of different machines doing different jobs," he wrote. "A single one will suffice. The engineering problem of producing various machines for different jobs is replaced by the office work of programming the universal machine to do these jobs."

Cracking the unbreakable code

Turing's introduction to the arcane world of codes, ciphers, and code-breaking started in 1938, when, on his return from Princeton University, he was approached by Alastair Denniston (1881–1961), director of the Government Code and Cipher School, to join a team of 59 cryptanalysts who were being recruited in the event of war. The task facing Turing and his colleagues was complex in the extreme. They had to crack the supposedly unbreakable codes generated by Germany's Enigma machine (see Feature, p. 35) and so open the door to decoding its military communications.

Working with fellow mathematician Gordon Welchman (1906–85), Turing's challenge was to design an electromechanical device, later christened Bombe, which could scan and, through the application of mathematical logic, analyze the vast amount of Enigma signal traffic Germany's armed forces were generating. The British Tabulating Machinery factory at nearby

BELOW:
Bletchley Park, a manor house 50 miles (80km) northwest of London, was the headquarters of the UK's code-breaking operations during World War II.

Letchworth built the first prototype Bombe, which went into service in May 1940. It was aptly codenamed "Victory." A second Bombe followed in August. By the end of the war, 9,000 operators were using 300 Turing-designed Bombes to process thousands of intelligence intercepts every day.

Even with the first Bombe designed, and more in the pipeline, the Enigma problem was far from solved. There was still no certain way of decoding the thousands upon thousands of messages the Germans were transmitting via the ciphers provided by their Enigma machines. Although the Bletchley cryptanalysts managed to crack the *Luftwaffe* Enigma code, the messages they decoded turned out to be mostly nursery rhymes sent out as practice transmissions. The real breakthrough was still to come.

ABOVE:

Wehrmacht troops using an Enigma machine to send and receive coded communications. The Germans' belief that Enigma was unbreakable gave the Allies a huge advantage.

Odd man out

With his shabby sports jacket, trousers held up with garden string, and fingernails bitten to the quick, Turing was the typical wartime nerd. Michael Paterson's *Voices of the Code Breakers* (2007) reveals Turing's many personal peculiarities at Bletchley Park, where he quickly earned the nickname "Prof." Fellow Cambridge mathematician Irving Good (1916–2009) noted, "In the first week of June each year, he would get a bad attack of hay fever, and he would cycle to the office wearing a gas mask to keep the pollen off. His bicycle had a fault; the chain would come off at regular intervals. Instead of having it repaired, he would count the number of times the pedals went round and would get off the bicycle in time to adjust the chain by hand. Another of his eccentricities was that he chained his mug to the radiator pipes to prevent it from being stolen."

Turing converted his savings into silver bars, believing that silver would retain its value even in the face of postwar economic fluctuations. He buried the bars in a carefully chosen spot—but was then never able to find the place again. Ann Harding, another of his colleagues, remembered another peculiarity: "Prof called me over to his table and handed me a sheet of figures. 'Please could you work these out for me?' he asked sheepishly." "I was appalled," she continued. "He was so obviously a very brilliant person, a lecturer in mathematics at Cambridge, and maths was not my strong subject. I had a good look and found it was all long division, plenty of it but simple. So I did it all and took it back to him. I said I couldn't understand why he wanted me to do it as I would have thought he would have done it in a flash. He looked rather embarrassed and said, 'Well, you see, I never did simple arithmetic.' At school, his maths master realized very quickly that he had a brilliant brain and put him straight onto advanced maths."

Persecution

There was one part of his life that Turing kept very much to himself. Good noted: "It was only after the war that we learned that he was a homosexual. It was lucky we didn't know about it early on, because if the powers-that-be had known, he might not have obtained security clearance and we might have lost the war." Turing's first love had been a fellow pupil at Sherborne School. Although the affair was never physically consummated, and the boy died of TB while both he and Turing were in the Sixth Form, there is little doubt that the memory of this ill-fated first love stayed with Turing for the rest of his life. When persecuted for his homosexuality after the war, Turing committed suicide.

FEATURE **Wheels within wheels**

The Enigma machine used three components that worked independently of each other. Twenty-six wires transmitted an electrical signal that passed through a plugboard and then through three rotors, which altered the direction of the input signal's direction as it passed through the encrypter. The rotors rotated independently while enciphering a message, so the left, middle, and right rotors never worked in tandem. In other words, the message was encrypted 26 times by 26 times by 26 times, meaning that someone seeking to decrypt the Enigma message would have to press 17,576 keys to find the starting point for the original message. Turing's Bombe decoding machine was capable of trying all 17,756 theoretical settings in just 20 minutes. It did this by performing electrically a chain of logical deductions based on a portion of plaintext, and rejecting those that produced a contradiction.

NAME: **Robert Watson-Watt**

NATIONALITY: British

BIRTH: April 13, 1892
DEATH: December 5, 1973

PROFESSION: Engineer

CATEGORY: Backroom hero

ACHIEVEMENT: He developed British radar and established Britain's first early warning system.

During the 1930s, the introduction of an effective radar network was imperative, given how vulnerable cities were to air attack. Every major power developed its own early warning system. Britain's was the brainchild of engineer Robert Watson-Watt, who realized that his thunderstorm-tracking system could be modified to detect enemy aircraft.

The German air force carried out the first sustained bombing campaign of a European capital when it attacked London during World War I. The fixed-wing aircraft of the period, however, were not able to transport a sizable payload of bombs from Germany to England, and so the job was done by Zeppelins—massive gas-filled blimps that were notoriously difficult to maneuver and whose huge hydrogen-filled frames made easy targets for interceptor aircraft. The raids, while not causing very much actual damage, awoke military planners to the vulnerability of cities to aerial attack.

By 1939, the range and carrying capacity of bombers meant that all British cities were within easy reach of the *Luftwaffe's* planes, which could carry sizable payloads of high-explosive and

incendiary bombs. The bombers could fly above
the range of anti-aircraft guns and drop their
bombs before fighters could be scrambled to
intercept them. What Britain needed was an
early warning system that would alert the RAF
to approaching German aircraft, and give its
fighters enough time to intercept them before
they dropped their bombs.

Storm hunter

Watson-Watt graduated in engineering at University
College Dundee, Scotland, in 1912, and took a job
in its physics department. It was there that he was
encouraged to study radio, an invention dating back
to the latter years of the 19th century, which was
being commercialized with some success by
Guglielmo Marconi (1874–1937). In 1899,
Marconi had realized that metallic objects reflected
radio waves, and that they could be used to create a
ship-to-ship detection system. The first practical
application of this discovery, however, was Christian Hülsmeyer's (1881–
1957) "Telemobiloscope" (patented in 1904), but the device suffered from
several shortcomings and was never developed commercially. Nevertheless,
many years later Watson-Watt generously recognized Hülsmeyer's
achievement when, at a Radar conference in 1953, he told him, "I am
the father of radar, whereas you are its grandfather."

ABOVE:
The Chain Home station
at Bawdsey on the Suffolk
coast was one of the first
radar facilities protecting
the British Isles from
enemy aircraft.

Having failed to join the War Office in 1916, Watson-Watt went to work
for the Meteorological Office, with the idea of using radio waves for the
long-distance detection of thunderstorms, which were a significant hazard to
the small aircraft of the day. In 1927, he became head of the Radio Research
Station Ditton Park, near Slough, UK, and in 1933, superintendent of the
radio department of the National Public Laboratory in Teddington, west
London. It was alongside his meteorological research in this second post that
he developed the equipment and many of the key concepts he would later
use in the development of military Radar.

A most secret trial

By the beginning of 1935, Watson-Watt had fully realized the military applications of his earlier work, and he sent a secret memo to the Air Ministry entitled "Detection and location of aircraft by radio methods." He arranged a demonstration of the technology using two receiving antennas about 6 miles (10km) from the BBC shortwave transmitter at Daventry, Northamptonshire. The equipment successfully detected a bomber that was being flown in the area. Armed with a patent for his "radio aircraft detector" and Air Ministry funding, Watson-Watt and his team continued their experiments, this time at Orford Ness, an isolated peninsula on the Suffolk Coast, where security would be less of a problem. When the initial detection range had increased from 16 miles (26km) to 60 miles (97km), the decision was taken that three air defense stations should be built around London.

BELOW:
By September 1940, radar coverage had been extended along the entire southern and eastern coastlines of the British Isles.

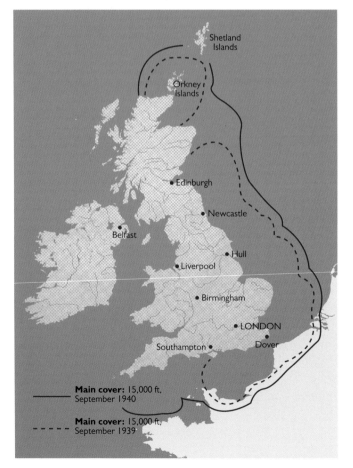

Main cover: 15,000 ft,
September 1940

Main cover: 15,000 ft,
September 1939

Invisible defense

The initial test of the world's first radar early warning system was a dismal failure, but not because of any technological shortcomings. The first three towers of what would become the "Chain Home" (CH) air defense system detected the aircraft, but the operators could not get the information to the fighter planes quickly enough. This problem was finally resolved by the implementation of Hugh Dowding's (1882–1970) integrated air defense system, of which Watson-Watt's radar posts were a key element, and which sent all information to a single control room, which then dispatched fighters to intercept enemy planes.

FEATURE **Radar on the move**

Even with the construction of the Chain Home network well advanced, Watson-Watt realized the need for airborne radar that would allow airborne interception (AI). The small fighter-borne system came into its own when the *Luftwaffe* switched tactics from trying to win air superiority with daytime raids during the Battle of Britain to the nighttime Blitz against British cities. Another application of airborne radar, known as ASV (air-to-surface vessel), allowed maritime patrol aircraft to locate and attack German naval forces, which led to the crippling of Hitler's U-boat fleet and ensured they could no longer attack shipping in British coastal waters. Separate Army and Navy projects included the Mobile Radio Unit, which was a truck-mounted version of a CH station that had a range of 60 miles (100km), and the Type 79Y ship-borne air defense system that had a detection range of between 30 and 50 miles (50–80km).

The first three CH stations were operational in 1937, and 17 more were under construction along the east and south coasts. At the outbreak of hostilities, CH had 19 working stations, which played a decisive role in the Battle of Britain. In 1939–40, the RAF had far too few Hurricanes and Spitfires at their disposal. Accurate detection and tracking of enemy aircraft with radar enabled the husbanding of aircraft and their direction to areas where they would counter the enemy most effectively. Without Watson-Watt's early warning system, the RAF might well have lost the Battle of Britain. By the end of the war, 50 CH stations provided both low- (500 feet; 150m) and high-altitude (1500 feet; 4.6km) cover to the whole of the British Isles.

ABOVE:
The Chain Home stations were part of Britain's integrated air defense system, which helped to ensure the defeat of the *Luftwaffe* air campaigns of 1940 and 1941.

NAME: **Barnes Wallis**

NATIONALITY: British

BIRTH: September 26, 1887

DEATH: October 30, 1979

PROFESSION: Inventor and engineer

CATEGORY: Backroom hero

ACHIEVEMENT: The designer of the "bouncing bomb" that was used in the Dambuster Raid.

Although Barnes Wallis is now widely remembered for one extraordinary weapon, the "bouncing bomb," which he designed to destroy the Axis powers' hydroelectric power infrastructure, he also made significant contributions to aircraft safety and performance with his innovative geodetic airframe and to the effectiveness of precision bombing with his "earthquake bombs."

This book features many entries that describe the activities and achievements of heroes who were in their 20s and 30s at the outbreak of war. Inventor and engineer Barnes Wallis, by contrast, was 52 when Britain declared war on Germany. He came from an earlier generation that had lived through World War I. It is often said that war, like life, is a young person's game, but there have always been exceptions. These men included Wallis' contemporaries, Field Marshal Bernard "Monty" Montgomery (1887–1976) and Prime Minister Winston Churchill, who could bring their vision and wisdom to bear on present difficulties, tempering innovation with experience and acting as figureheads who might inspire their younger subordinates and provide much-needed focus within such a vast and multifaceted operation.

In the frame

Barnes Wallis began his career in marine engineering in 1905. In 1913
he joined British aviation company Vickers, who would later employ his
younger contemporary, Spitfire designer Reginald Mitchell (see pp. 24–27).
Wallis first worked on what was then the cutting-edge of aviation
technology: Britain's R-Series airships. He designed the lightweight
framework that held the vulnerable gasbags of the R100 and her sister ship,
the R101. But the future was not with lighter-than-air aircraft that were
prone to catastrophic failures—the R101 crashed in France in October
1930, effectively ending Britain's airship program; the Hindenburg disaster
seven years later marked the disappearance of large passenger airships from
world skies for many decades.

The future was not in lighter-than-air rigid
aircraft but in heavier-than-air fixed-wing
aircraft, and it was to the design and construction
of aircraft fuselage and wings that Barnes Wallis
applied the skills he had learned in designing
lightweight airship frames. Vickers applied his
geodetic (also geodesic) airframes to Rex Pierson's
(1891–1948) Wellington mid-range bomber, and
to Wallis' own Wellesley light bomber. The
duralumin latticework frame created a light but
very strong structure that was resilient to major
combat damage. Although whole parts of the fuselage could be destroyed,
the geodetic structure preserved the load-bearing integrity of the whole,
allowing seriously damaged planes to return to base.

ABOVE:

The fuselage of a bomber
with Wallis' geodetic
airframe exposed; the
revolutionary design enabled
badly damaged aircraft to
remain in one piece and
return to base.

Booms and busts

Another advantage that the older Barnes Wallis had over someone younger,
such as Reginald Jones (see pp. 20–23), was that he had long-established
contacts in military and government circles. He had elaborated his own
distinctive ideas about how to defeat Germany with a highly focused
bombing campaign. In 1941 he sent "A Note on a Method of Attacking
the Axis Powers" to one hundred of his military and political contacts.
The principal tactic he advocated was to attack and destroy Germany's

BELOW:

The barrel-shaped bomb skipped over the dam's defenses.

BOTTOM:

The bomb sank to the base of the inner wall, where it exploded, breaching the dam.

energy infrastructure, including coal and oil fields, hydroelectric dams, and underground oil storage tanks. He concluded, "If their destruction or paralysis can be accomplished, they offer a means of rendering the enemy utterly incapable of continuing to prosecute the war." Wallis had also begun to devise new types of super-bomb (see Feature, p. 43) to attack major industrial, military, and energy installations, but his first designs were so large that no existing aircraft were able to carry them.

Nevertheless, Wallis' privately circulated paper made its mark, because it led to the establishment of the Aerial Attacks on Dams Committee, charged

with examining the feasibility of attacking hydroelectric installations in Germany and Italy. The result was "Operation Chastise," better-known to generations of British film audiences and TV viewers as the Dambuster Raid after the movie, *The Dam Busters* (1955), which immortalized the attack on three dams in the Ruhr Valley, Germany's industrial heartland. On the evening of May 16, 1943, 19 Lancaster bombers from 617 Squadron, made up of aircrew from Britain, Canada, Australia, and New Zealand, set off for their targets, carrying Wallis' specially designed "bouncing bombs."

If you've ever skimmed a flat stone over the water, you will immediately grasp the principle that Wallis was using to get his bomb over the dams' defenses, and get it to just the right position so that a relatively small charge could demolish a massive reinforced steel and concrete structure. The bombers flew in fast and low, dropping their payload at 60 feet (18m) above the water. The spinning barrel-shaped bomb bounced on the surface of the water several times, jumping over antitorpedo

Manmade earthquakes

Much of the bombing during the war was "area bombardment," which targeted a whole city or district in the hope of destroying critical installations. Precision bombing was only developed toward the end of the war, making the targeting of specific facilities possible. But even if deployed accurately, the payloads carried by Allied bombers were not able to destroy well-protected installations. To address this problem, Barnes Wallis designed two massive "earthquake bombs": the 6-ton "Tallboy" and the 10-ton "Grand Slam," which could penetrate the deepest wartime bunkers. Combined with new precision bombing techniques, the bombs were used to destroy the V-2 flying bomb factory, sink a heavily armored German battleship, damage the concrete U-boat pens at St. Nazaire on the French coast, and destroy a railway tunnel in central France shortly after the D-Day landings, preventing Panzer reinforcements reaching Normandy by train.

ABOVE:
Barnes Wallis designed weapons to penetrate the strongest underground bunkers, but initially no Allied plane was large enough to carry his "earthquake bombs."

nets, hit the dam face, and sank down, detonating at a depth where the blast wave would create the maximum amount of damage.

Despite heavy casualties among the attacking planes, two of the targets, the Möhne and Edersee dams, were breached, causing catastrophic flooding, but the third target, the Sorpe dam, only suffered minor damage. Wallis wrote, "I feel a blow has been struck at Germany from which she cannot recover for several years." Unfortunately, by the end of the June, the Germans had managed to restore water and electricity supplies.

Espionage heroes

Espionage is a dirty, dishonorable business, perhaps never more so than in wartime, when so much is at stake. In the world of fictional World War II espionage, there are two types of spy: the "good," brave, honorable, and trustworthy secret agents, who risked their lives to serve king and country, and the "bad," dishonorable, double-dealing, double-crossing agents, whose motivations were money or adventure. But the reality of espionage during World War II was far more ambiguous. Honorable men and women could be sometimes persuaded to do dishonorable things, on the grounds that the ends justify the means. Conversely, dishonorable men and women sometimes did the right thing. More interesting in their ambiguity are men and women who may have been career criminals, and double agents who worked for the Allied cause and did the right thing for all the wrong reasons.

NAME: **Eddie Chapman**

NATIONALITY: British

BIRTH: November 16, 1914
DEATH: December 11, 1997

PROFESSION: Spy

CATEGORY: Espionage hero

ACHIEVEMENT: As a double agent, he was part of British Intelligence's web of deceit used against the Germans.

A violent career criminal, Eddie Chapman found himself in German hands during the war and immediately offered them his services as a traitor and saboteur. Betrayed to MI5 by decrypted Enigma messages, he was captured by the British, changed sides, and became a double agent in occupied Europe.

In the murky world of wartime espionage, it is sometimes difficult to distinguish friend from foe. Alongside the truly admirable, heroic men and women, who risked and often sacrificed their lives to serve their countries and combat the evils of Nazism, there were men and women whose motivations were not quite so pure and praiseworthy. Espionage, by its very nature, requires deceit and duplicity, but these are thought to be admissible in the service of a just cause. We know that the secret agents that went into occupied Europe were sometimes expected to act dishonorably, but we forgive them if they did so for honorable motives, and as long as they did not cross the line that would make them as bad as the Nazis they were fighting. This is particularly true in view of the immense risks each operative willingly exposed themselves to.

Eddie Chapman represents the second type of secret agent, who spied for the Allies during World War II. By background, training, and inclination, he was a violent career criminal who had served time in prison. Had British Military Intelligence appealed to his finer nature, sense of duty, and patriotism, they would have been sorely disappointed, but they knew their man, and they offered him what he wanted most: money. An MI5 officer made the following assessment: "Chapman loved himself, loved adventure, and loved his country, probably in that order." He is representative of a breed of men and women with very specialized skills—and in peacetime, those skills had landed them in prison. But in wartime their talents were directed in an altogether different direction, enabling then to serve their countries, often in spite of themselves.

A checkered criminal career

Chapman was an ill-disciplined child, if not a full-blown juvenile delinquent, who played truant from school. In 1931, aged 17, he joined the British Army, but quickly got bored of military routine. He went absent without leave, hiding out with a girl he had met in London. Arrested by the military police, he served three months in military prison and was dishonorably discharged from the army. Upon his release, Chapman gravitated toward London's criminal underworld. He started small with petty thefts, frauds, and forgeries, which landed him in civilian prison for the first time. Unreformed, he graduated to safe-cracking as a member of the "Jelly Gang"—so called because they used gelignite to blow safes open.

His 1942 MI5 mugshots show a tough but, by the standards of the day, masculine, dashing man of 33, which accounted for his other "line of work": blackmailing wealthy society women with whom he had had affairs. Parts of this description tallies with several of the qualities of Ian Fleming's (1908–64) James Bond, who exploited every human weakness to fulfill his missions. But Chapman was no 007—for one thing, he was always getting caught. Just before the war, he was arrested for robbing a Cooperative Society (savings and loans association) office in Edinburgh, Scotland, but managed to escape to Jersey, one of the Channel Islands between England and France. About to be apprehended by the police for his Scottish heist, he managed to escape, but on the very same night was arrested while trying to commit a burglary. He probably realized that serving a short sentence on Jersey would spare him the much longer prison term he would have received had he been returned to the mainland for trial.

Double turncoat

Occupied by the Nazi forces in 1940, the Channel Islands were the only part of the British Isles that were occupied by the Germans. Along with this small chunk of Britain and its hostile population, the Germans got one Eddie Chapman, serving time for burglary in the island's prison. He promptly offered his services to the Germans as a spy in exchange for his freedom. The *Abwehr*, German military intelligence (see Feature on the next page), trained him as a secret agent and saboteur. In December 1942, he was flown back to England armed with a radio, pistol, cyanide capsule, and £1,000 in cash, with orders to sabotage the de Havilland aircraft factory in Hatfield, Essex.

Thanks to Enigma decrypts, MI5 already knew of Chapman's mission and were waiting to arrest him at his designated point of arrival, but Chapman had problems exiting the aircraft and landed miles away from his intended target. A manhunt to find him proved unnecessary because Chapman immediately surrendered to the police and offered his services to British Intelligence as a double agent. Henceforth, he would be known as agent "Zigzag" and be run by the Double-Cross System (see Feature, p. 83).

ABOVE:

The Channel Islands, between France and England, were the only part of the British Isles occupied by the Nazis during World War II.

Little Fritz

In order to maintain Chapman's identity as a German agent, the British faked a sabotage attack on the de Havilland factory that fooled German air reconnaissance photographs. MI5 then arranged to return him to his German handlers via neutral Lisbon. Chapman was awarded the Iron Cross and the rank of *Oberleutnant*, received 110,000 Reichmarks and a yacht for his services to Germany, and earned the affectionate nickname "Little Fritz" from his colleagues. He was then dispatched to Oslo in occupied Norway to train operatives at an *Abwehr* spy school. In 1944, after D-Day, the Germans sent him back to England to report on V-1 damage. Chapman soon returned to his old criminal ways in London. To save embarrassment, MI5 thought it best to dismiss him, giving him £6,000 and a full pardon for his prewar crimes in exchange for his silence about his work as a secret agent.

FEATURE **Chapman's women**

Like the fictional James Bond, Chapman seems to have had a girl in every major city. When he was in Oslo, he began a relationship with Dagmar Lahlum (1922–99), a member of the Norwegian resistance. Although he had told her that he was a British double agent, she was unable to prove Chapman's true identity and after the war was sentenced to six months in prison for collaborating with an enemy officer. While he was having his affair with Lahlum, he was engaged to another girl in London. After the war, however, he abandoned both Norwegian mistress and English fiancée and returned to his prewar lover, Betty Farmer, whom he had met on Jersey. Chapman got a less-than-well-deserved happy ending, running businesses in Italy and Ireland until his death of a heart attack aged 83.

NAME: **Eric Erickson**

NATIONALITY: American and Swedish

BIRTH: ca. 1890 (exact date unknown)
DEATH: January 24, 1983

PROFESSION: Oil executive

CATEGORY: Espionage hero

ACHIEVEMENT: He aided Allied attacks on the Reich's synthetic oil industry, starving Germany's war machine of vital fuel.

As befits a spy, not that much is known about what American-born Swedish oil executive Eric Erickson actually did during World War II. Was he the kingpin who single-handedly destroyed Germany's synthetic oil industry? Or was he a late convert to the Allied cause who was trying to save his own skin?

The world of espionage is, of course, a web of secrets and lies, often spun by intelligence agencies themselves to conceal their activities from friend and foe alike. These secrets are usually cleared up a few decades after the event or, at least, when the historical fallout has had a chance to settle. But there are a few certain facts about Eric Erickson's wartime activities. We know that he did something significant for the Allied cause because he was praised by both Presidents Eisenhower (1890–1969) and Truman (1884–1972), but there are several versions of the Erickson story: his own; the romanticized Hollywood version told in Paramount's *The Counterfeit Traitor* (1962), starring William Holden (1918–81); and the objective "truth," which is somewhere out there, waiting to be uncovered.

Erickson: the official story

In some spy cases, even 70 years on, historical
clarity can be a rare commodity. In "How an
American Nazi Collaborator Became an Allied
Spy" (*The Atlantic*, September 18, 2013),
American historian of espionage Stephen Talty
tried to sort out fact from fiction, but he was
forced to admit: "Erickson is too large and
slippery a character for me to be convinced
I know everything about him."

ABOVE:
Erickson (portrayed here
by William Holden) won
the confidence of the Nazi
regime, which granted him
privileged access to its
synthetic oil manufacturing
and storage facilities.

Like Talty, I gleaned Erickson's official biography from his obituary in
The New York Times for January 25, 1983. According to *The Times*, Erickson
was born in 1890 in the USA, the son of Swedish immigrants. He fought
in World War I, after which he moved to Texas to work in the oil business.
In 1924, he emigrated to Sweden, where he set up his own oil company
and became a Swedish citizen in the mid-1930s. Sweden remained neutral
during World War II and was therefore unoccupied by either side. In 1939,
Erickson offered to spy for the USA, specifically to reveal Axis facilities for
manufacturing and storing synthetic oil that the Allied air forces would
later target during the war.

In order to establish his cover, Erickson pretended to be a committed
Nazi supporter. He was a regular visitor to Berlin during the war, where
he was welcomed by the highest echelons of the Nazi elite. He became
friends with Hermann Göring, head of the *Luftwaffe*, and Heinrich
Himmler (1900–45), the leader of the SS. Himmler went so far as to
provide Erickson with accreditation that allowed him free access to all
Germany's synthetic oil installations.

Erickson: cracks in the mask

When investigating Erickson's story, Talty uncovered several discrepancies
between the official account and the historical record, the first being
Erickson's real age. Instead of being old enough to have served in the
American Expeditionary Forces that sailed to Europe in 1917, Erickson was
at least seven years younger than his stated age. As a teenager of 17 or 18, he

could not have been, as he later claimed, an intelligence officer on the Western Front. He was more likely finishing high school and enjoying his freshman year at Cornell in 1917–18.

The second, and to my mind, much greater discrepancy uncovered by Talty is the date when Erickson offered his service to the OSS, America's wartime intelligence service. Erickson claimed that he had done so at the outbreak of war, because he considered Hitler to be insane and he "wanted to crush him." Sound sentiments for a patriotic American, even though in 1939 the USA was still two years away from joining the war. But according to OSS records, Erickson started passing information to them not in 1939 but in 1942—by which time Hitler was failing in Russia and the Japanese advance in the Pacific had been halted. It was a good time for a thoughtful businessman, with considerable business interests in the Reich, to reconsider his postwar options.

OPPOSITE:
By depriving Germany of vital fuel for its military machine, the bombing campaign targeting oil was a significant factor in the Allied victory.

Nazi collaborator or secret patriot?

Erickson's late conversion to the Allied cause might mean that far from feigning a love of Hitler, Erickson had enthusiastically embraced Nazism sometime between Hitler's rise to power in 1933 and the outbreak of war. The ease with which he obtained access to top-secret installations would certainly make more sense had Erickson been an early convert and trusted collaborator, one who was not only a valued business partner but had also offered to rationalize and increase Germany's production of synthetic oil (see Feature, opposite).

In Erickson's defense, Talty cited his love affair with an OSS agent who died during the war, as well as a letter to an African-American correspondent in which he had expressed the following very un-Nazi sentiment: "A man's race, his religion, or his color has in my life made no difference to me at all. All that I judge people by is their decency." I may be less charitable or trusting than Mr. Talty, and I remain unconvinced. Erickson did make a major contribution to the Allied war effort, but was it out of patriotic zeal or to escape being condemned as a collaborator after Germany lost the war?

FEATURE **Oil wars**

Hitler may have had one of the most advanced war machines the world had ever seen, but he lacked the one crucial commodity without which a Panzer tank and a Messerschmitt fighter are just so many piles of junk: oil. One reason Hitler turned his back on the conquest of Britain in 1941 and attacked the USSR was that he wanted to seize the valuable Caucasus oil fields, which, alongside those in the USA and Near East, were among the most productive. His failure to secure a supply of crude oil meant that Germany's war machine was increasingly dependent of the production of synthetic oil. Thanks to his high-level SS clearance, Erickson was able to visit and study all of Germany's synthetic oil installations, relaying the information to the OSS, which in turn organized for the facilities to be bombed. After the war, *Luftwaffe* Field Marshal Erhard Milch (1892–1972), referring to the Allied campaign against German oil production, admitted that, "The British left us with deep and bleeding wounds, but the Americans stabbed us in the heart."

NAME: Christine Granville

NATIONALITY: Polish and British

BIRTH: May 1, 1908
DEATH: June 15, 1952

PROFESSION: SOE operative

CATEGORY: Espionage hero

ACHIEVEMENT: She took part in SIS and SOE operations in eastern Europe and Egypt, and particularly in occupied France.

Many women volunteered to work as Special Operations Executive (SOE) agents in occupied Europe, and many paid the ultimate price in the service of the Allied cause. Christine Granville was one of the first of these female operatives. She was active in eastern Europe, Egypt, and France, and miraculously survived until the end of the war.

After the less-than-honorable Eddie Chapman (pp. 46–49) and Erik Erickson (see the preceding entry), we come to a secret agent who was a truly inspirational wartime hero, thanks to her determination to oppose Nazism and free her native Poland from foreign occupation. Christine Granville, *née* Krystyna Skarbek, was one of the first female operatives to be recruited by the SOE. She is noteworthy in that she operated covertly in several of the most difficult wartime theaters from 1940, and managed to survive unscathed until the end of the war.

Her postwar career, however, was much less fortunate. Like many Poles who had fought alongside the Allies to defeat Hitler, she became stateless and penniless when Poland ended up on the wrong side of Joseph Stalin's (1878–1953)

Iron Curtain in 1945. A life so full of heroism and adventure ended tragically at the age of 44, when the much-decorated Granville was murdered in the lobby of a seedy London hotel by a rejected lover— another stark contrast with both Chapman and Erickson, who managed to profit from their wartime activities, and lived comfortably until they died of old age.

Into enemy lands

The daughter of an impoverished Polish aristocrat, Granville married a diplomat and was living overseas when Germany invaded Poland, triggering England and France's declaration of war. The couple made their way to London to support the Allied cause, and Granville joined Britain's Secret Intelligence Service (SIS). Her first mission was to Hungary, a German ally, and to neighboring occupied Poland in December 1939. While she was in Warsaw, she tried persuade her Jewish-born mother to leave the country but she refused, a decision that led to her death at the hands of the *Gestapo*.

Being in her native Warsaw was dangerous for Granville, who was recognized and accosted in a café by a former acquaintance. Her first mission also took her to Hungary, where she met an old friend, Andrzej Kowerski (1912–88), a Polish army officer who later joined SOE under the alias "Andrew Kennedy." Together, they collected intelligence and helped servicemen to escape occupied Poland. In January 1941, the pair were arrested by the *Gestapo* in Budapest, but Granville managed to engineer their release by faking an attack of TB. They fled Hungary through the Balkans and Turkey and made their way to the British protectorate of Egypt.

ABOVE:
One of the new technologies invented before the First World War but perfected in time for the Second, radio was used to transmit both information and disinformation.

Kicking her heels in Cairo

Granville and Kowerski presented themselves at SOE HQ in Cairo, confident that they would be given new assignments in occupied Europe. They were shocked to learn that they were under suspicion by the Polish government-in-exile in London, and that SOE was under instructions not to send them back to the Balkans or Poland. Although the pair were cleared in 1943 thanks to the intervention of the head of SOE, Granville remained bored and underemployed in Cairo for three years. To occupy her time, she trained as a wireless operator and did a parachuting course with the RAF in Haifa, Palestine. In March 1944, she applied to be sent back to Hungary as a wireless operator, but a month later the mission was canceled. Fortunately as it turned out, because a much more important assignment came up as a courier in the South of France.

The formidable "Madame Pauline"

It was the closing 12 months of the Europe war, although no one in the spring of 1944 knew how long it would take to defeat Germany. And the Germans themselves had far from given up. The *Gestapo*, assisted by French collaborators, were extremely active in France, capturing and executing many SOE operatives and scoring successes against the French Resistance. Granville, given the false identity of Jacqueline Armand, and the codename "Madame Pauline," was parachuted into France a month after the D-Day landings. She worked for SOE operative and Resistance leader Francis Cammaerts (1916–2006), who controlled the Resistance from the Riviera to the Rhône Valley and as far north as Grenoble at the foot of the French Alps.

Granville was sent to the Italian border, where one of the high Alpine passes was guarded by Polish soldiers who had been conscripted into the German

---

FEATURE   **"Churchill's Secret Army"**

"The Baker Street Irregulars" and the "Ministry of Ungentlemanly Warfare" were two of the unofficial names used to refer to the Special Operations Executive (SOE), a shadowy organization that conducted a secret war against the Axis powers. Officially, it was given the anodyne titles of the "Joint Technical Board" or the "Inter-Service Research Bureau." SOE was established by Minister of Economic Warfare Hugh Dalton (1887–1962) in July 1940. Its mission was to conduct espionage, sabotage, and reconnaissance in occupied Europe, the Near East, and North Africa, and to support local resistance movements with arms, money, training, and personnel. In the darkest days of the Battle of Britain, it also organized a secret resistance army that would have fought a German invasion and occupation. At its peak, SOE oversaw 13,000 operatives, about 3,200 of whom were women. They stayed in touch with London via B2 radio sets, as well as through BBC broadcasts.

ABOVE:
A U.S. Navy Hellcat fighter plane launches from the USS *Kasaan Bay* during the invasion of southern France in August 1944.

army. She persuaded them to change sides and to disable the heavy guns that guarded the pass. But Granville's finest hour came when her boss, Cammaerts, fellow SOE agent Alexander "Xan" Fielding (1918–91), and a French officer were arrested by the *Gestapo* days before the Allied landings in the South of France. Bluffing on an empty hand, she used a mixture of threats and the promise of postwar Allied protection, backed up by a two-million-franc bribe, to persuade Albert Schenck, a French collaborator working for the *Gestapo*, to arrange for the men's escape just hours before they were due to be executed. For these, and other acts of extraordinary heroism, she was awarded the French *Croix de Guerre*, the British civil decoration the George Medal, and an OBE (Officer of the Most Excellent Order of the British Empire).

NAME:	**Virginia Hall**
NATIONALITY:	American
BIRTH:	April 6, 1906
DEATH:	July 8, 1982
PROFESSION:	SOE/OSS agent
CATEGORY:	Espionage hero
ACHIEVEMENT:	She established an SOE network in France and acted as liaison between the French Resistance and Allied forces.

On the *Gestapo's* most-wanted list, American SOE operative Virginia Hall joined the war against Hitler well before her own government. She started her career as a secret agent, employed by the SOE, and then worked for the OSS in 1944, organizing French Resistance forces and liaising with the advancing Allies after D-Day.

The U.S. government joined the war against the Axis powers after the surprise attack on Pearl Harbor, but many private American citizens, such as the fictional Rick Blaine, played by Humphrey Bogart (1899–1957) in the movie *Casablanca* (1942) and the hero of the *Indiana Jones* franchise, joined the fight against Nazism long before 1941. As citizens of the world's most powerful nation, which the Nazis and their allies did not initially at least seek to antagonize, they were ideally placed to act as secret agents working for the British.

Virginia Hall came from a privileged New England background, graduating from prestigious academic institutions that included Radcliffe College (now part of Harvard) and Barnard College (now part of Columbia). She majored in

European languages, and traveled to Europe to study French and German at Paris' Sorbonne and Vienna's Konsularakademie in 1926. She had ambitions to join the Foreign Service but did not do well enough in the State Department entrance examination, so decided to return to Europe to gain firsthand experience in the U.S. consular service. She obtained a clerical post in Warsaw in 1931, and two years later was in Istanbul, Turkey, when something happened that was to change the course of her life. She lost part of her leg in a hunting accident and thereafter had to wear a wooden prosthesis that she nicknamed "Cuthbert."

After convalescing in the USA, she was posted to Venice, where she was told that she could never hope for a career in the foreign service because she had lost her leg—an extraordinary decision, in light of what Hall would achieve during the war. After a final posting in Tallin, Estonia, Hall resigned from the foreign service in 1939 and went to Paris to consider her future.

La dame qui boite

At the outbreak of war, the indomitable Hall volunteered to be an ambulance driver in the French army. When the French capitulated in June 1940, she found herself in the Vichy-controlled southern half of France. As an American, Hall was not an enemy alien and was therefore free to travel to London, where she got a job at the American Embassy. During a social function, Hall met Vera Atkins (1908–2000) of SOE's F-(France) Section, who recognized in her not just a useful linguist but also a person who could handle the extreme strain of undercover work. SOE trained her and sent her to Vichy in August 1941, assigning her the cover of a reporter for the *New York Post*. While maintaining her journalistic cover and writing regular articles for the *Post*, Hall, using a number of aliases, spent the next 14 months organizing Resistance networks, helping British airmen to escape capture, acting as a courier for other SOE agents, and providing supplies for clandestine presses producing forged documents.

BELOW:
In addition to working with SOE agents, the French Resistance depended on supplies of weapons, radios, cash, and forged documents dropped by air by the British.

When the Allies invaded North Africa in the fall of 1942, the Germans occupied southern France, until then nominally under the control of the Vichy government. Hall, "the lady with a limp," was number one on German intelligence's most-wanted list. She had to escape, her only route being south into neutral but hostile Spain, crossing the Pyrenees in winter on foot. She was allowed to proceed to London after a few weeks in detention. She requested a new French posting, but it was considered too dangerous for her to return to France, so she was instead sent to Madrid, where she remained bored and underemployed until 1944, when she returned to London and requested a return to fieldwork.

RIGHT:
The rate at which Resistance agents were betrayed and captured persuaded Hall's superiors not to post her once again in France.

A return to France

As SOE was not keen to send Hall back to France, she applied to join the OSS (see Feature, opposite), which was looking to recruit personnel to prepare for Operation Overlord (the D-Day landings). In March 1944, she was taken to the Brittany coast by motor launch (because her artificial leg prevented her from being dropped by parachute), and from there traveled to central France. She took on the persona of an old farm worker called Marcelle Montagne, but under her codename of "Diane" she helped train three battalions of resistance fighters, organized sabotage operations and guerrilla attacks by French partisans, and after the D-Day landings linked up

FEATURE **Spying for Uncle Sam**

Before the war, the U.S. government had an ambivalent attitude to foreign intelligence gathering. In 1929 Secretary of State Henry Stimson (1867–1950) shut down the State Department's codebreaking division run by Herbert Yardley (1889–1958), on the grounds that "Gentlemen don't read each other's mail." President Roosevelt, concerned that the USA did not have a centralized intelligence capacity, asked William Donovan (1883–1959) to establish an intelligence service modeled on Britain's MI6 and SOE. Donovan set up an initial organization with the help of the British in July 1941, but he faced opposition from the existing intelligence agencies. The deficiencies of U.S. intelligence were exposed by the attack on Pearl Harbor, which Donovan, with the British, tried to make good by helping with information, equipment, and training for American personnel. On June 13, 1942, a presidential order established the OSS to coordinate espionage activities in enemy territory.

ABOVE:
Women featured prominently among Resistance fighters and SOE operatives. Pictured here is "Nicole," who captured 25 Germans in Chartres in 1944.

with a covert commando unit, made up of agents from the SOE, OSS, and Free French intelligence bureau. She acted as a radio operator and courier, located drop zones for the RAF for supplies and commandos, and continued to pass intelligence information on German troop movements until Allied troops reached her in September 1944.

Whereas others might have rested on their laurels, Hall, who received an MBE from Britain and the Distinguished Service Cross from the USA, joined the newly formed CIA, where she worked until the mandatory retirement age of 60.

NAME: **Knut Haukelid**

NATIONALITY: American and Norwegian

BIRTH: May 17, 1911
DEATH: March 8, 1994

PROFESSION: Norwegian commando

CATEGORY: Espionage hero

ACHIEVEMENT: Haukelid and his team ensured that Hitler would not be able to build his own nuclear weapons.

American-born Knut Haukelid was one of the six-strong Gunnerside commando team that destroyed the Norsk Hydro heavy water plant in Vemork, Norway. He also prevented significant reserves of heavy water from reaching Germany when he sank the *SF Hydro* ferry.

During World War II, many events were so noteworthy that they were later dramatized in film. There was *The Longest Day* (1962) about the D-Day landings, and *The Dam Busters* (1955) about Operation Chastise (see Barnes Wallis, pp. 40–43). But few military operations have merited two movies, a TV documentary, and a shelf-full of history books. Operation Gunnerside, however, so much caught the public imagination that it spawned two feature films, *Operation Swallow: The Battle for Heavy Water* (1948), featuring several of the original participants in the raid, including Knut Haukelid, and *The Heroes of Telemark* (1965), in which Richard Harris (1930–2002) took the role of Knut Straud, a fictional character based on Haukelid and other commandos in the team.

Hitler's A-bomb

The entries on Enrico Fermi (pp. 12–15) and Robert Oppenheimer (pp. 28–31) feature the Manhattan Project—the most secret weapons program of World War II, and by far its most ambitious and expensive. Manhattan had its German counterpart, *Uranverein* (Uranium Club), which sought to build on German discoveries in nuclear fission to create a first-generation nuclear weapon. Unlike Manhattan, which developed both uranium and plutonium bombs, *Uranverein* concentrated on a plutonium device. Like the Americans, the Germans were working on a nuclear reactor to enrich the uranium and turn it into weapons-grade plutonium.

Fermi had succeeded in creating fissile material by using graphite as the moderator to slow the neutrons released by the uranium in the reactor, but the Germans opted for another method, using heavy water as the moderator in their reactor. Heavy water—D_2O, rather than H_2O—is denser than ordinary water because it contains deuterium (heavy hydrogen) rather than hydrogen. Heavy water occurs naturally in regular water, but in such minute quantities that it has to be separated from it by electrolysis or other elaborate and time-consuming chemical processes.

ABOVE:
The isolated Norsk Hydro plant in Norway was the only facility in Europe capable of producing enough heavy water for Hitler's A-bomb project.

In 1935, the Norwegian firm Norsk Hydro built the world's first commercial heavy water plant at Vemork, 114 miles (183km) west of Oslo. Even at full capacity, the plant could only produce 22lb (10kg) of heavy water per month, but the Germans required far more for their nuclear weapons program. When Germany occupied Norway in April 1940, it took control of the plant and immediately increased production. All existing stores of heavy water, however, had already been removed so as not to fall into German hands (see Feature, opposite).

A disastrous start

Operation Gunnerside was not the first attempt to destroy the Norsk Hydro plant, but the third in a series of raids planned by SOE to end heavy water production. The first two, Operations Grouse and Freshman, were attempted in October–November 1942. Operation Grouse—the insertion of four SOE-trained Norwegian commandos near the plant, was a success. With the commandos in place, SOE dispatched two gliders carrying a demolition team of British Royal Engineers. Tragically, due to poor weather conditions and equipment failures, both gliders crash landed. With many of the crew dead or injured, the survivors were quickly captured by the Germans, tortured by the *Gestapo*, and later executed. The four-man Norwegian team, however, managed to escape capture and remained in the area.

Third time's a charm

Undeterred, SOE immediately started to plan a third attempt, codenamed "Operation Gunnerside," this time made up of six Norwegian commandos, including Haukelid. They parachuted in near the plant and joined up with the original four-man Norwegian team. On the night of February 27–28, 1943, the commandos successfully passed through minefields, avoided patrols and guards, and penetrated the plant by crawling through an access tunnel and then a window. The plant itself was deserted apart from a Norwegian caretaker, who was only too happy to assist his compatriots.

The team placed explosive charges on the electrolysis chambers, set the fuses, and made good their escape. They destroyed the vital equipment needed to extract the heavy water, along with a 1,102lb (500kg) store of the precious liquid. Despite a manhunt involving 3,000 German troops, five of the commandos skied to freedom to neighboring Sweden, two went to ground in Oslo, and four others, including Haukelid, stayed behind to work with local partisans.

Although the plant resumed operations within a few months, it became the target of heavy USAAF bombing raids. The Germans, fearing that it was just a matter of time before the plant and its stores were destroyed, decided to transport the most critical equipment and remaining heavy water to Germany. The first leg of the journey was by the ferry *SF Hydro* across Lake Tinnsjø. Haukelid, who was the only trained commando in the area at the time, was ordered to destroy the shipment before it left Norway. He slipped aboard the ferry and placed a timed bomb deep inside its keel. The bomb went off at around midnight, when *Hydro* was in the middle of the lake. She sank in deep water, taking with her any chance that the Germans would ever succeed in enriching enough plutonium to make a nuclear bomb.

ABOVE:
The threat posed by U.S. bombers persuaded the Germans to remove equipment and stores of heavy water from Vemork.

FEATURE   **Operation Eau Lourde**

In order to stop the 408lb (185kg) store of heavy water produced by Norsk Hydro from falling into enemy hands when the Germans occupied Norway, French military intelligence sent three agents to Vemork to organize its removal to France. Axel Aubert (1873–1943), Director-General of Norsk Hydro, agreed to "lend" the heavy water to the French government for the duration of hostilities, knowing full well that he was risking his life should Germany win the war. The French managed to avoid agents of the *Abwehr* in Norway and transported the heavy water to Oslo, from where it was shipped to Perth, Scotland, and then on to France. When France itself fell, physicist Frédéric Joliot-Curie (1900–58) hid the water in a vault in the Banque de France and then in a prison before moving it secretly to Bordeaux, from where it was shipped to Britain aboard the *SS Broompark*.

NAME: **Noor-un-Nisa Inayat Khan**

NATIONALITY: Indian and American

BIRTH: January 2, 1914
DEATH: September 13, 1944

PROFESSION: SOE agent

CATEGORY: Espionage hero

ACHIEVEMENT: Given the most dangerous posting in France, when captured she resisted her captors' efforts to break her.

Although considered temperamentally unsuited to undercover work by those who had trained her to be the first female wireless operator to be sent to France by SOE, Noor-un-Nisa Inayat Khan surprised both her colleagues in London and her German captors in the *Sicherheitsdienst* (SD; the Nazi intelligence service) by her strength and resilience.

If asked to imagine the ideal female candidate to work as a secret agent behind enemy lines during World War II, we might think of the tomboyish, Polish-born Christine Granville (pp. 54–57), the formidable Virginia Hall (pp. 58–61), with her artificial leg nicknamed "Cuthbert," or the larger-than-life Nancy Wake (pp. 106–109), who killed a man with a single karate-chop. The achievements of all three women are comparable to anything done by their male counterparts. Noor-un-Nisa Inayat Khan was cast in a completely different mold. She was the daughter of an Indian father, Inayat Khan (1882–1927), a classical musician from a noble Muslim house, who was the founder of the Sufi Order in the West, and an American mother, Ora Ray Baker (1892–1949), who had married against her family's wishes and adopted the Muslim name Ameena Begum.

Cosmopolitan, cultured, and spiritual

Inayat and Ora Ray met and married in the USA but soon left for Europe. Khan, the eldest of four children, was born in Russia in 1914. Just before the outbreak of World War I, the family moved to London, where Khan spent the first seven years of her life. There followed a move to Paris in 1921, where the Khan family settled in a western suburb of the city in a house gifted to them by the Sufi movement. After Inayat's early death at the age of 45, while on a visit to India, the 13-year-old Khan became responsible for the care of her mother and three younger siblings.

Her studies and interests reflected her cosmopolitan, cultured, and spiritual upbringing. In 1931 she studied the piano and harp at the École Normale de Musique and enrolled at the Sorbonne to study child psychology; she wrote stories for French radio, newspapers, and magazines; and in 1939 published *Twenty Jataka Tales*, a compendium of Buddhist stories for children. She spoke several languages fluently, including French and English, and was deeply influenced by her father's philosophy of universal peace and brotherhood.

ABOVE:
During WWII, women played an important part in the Allied war effort, and not just in an auxiliary capacity as nurses or members of the WAAF, but in frontline roles as secret agents working behind enemy lines.

An unlikely spy

When the Germans invaded France, the family fled to Bordeaux, from where they boarded a ship for England. In November 1940, Khan enlisted in the Women's Auxiliary Air Force (WAAF), using the anglicized Nora instead of her Muslim name. She trained as a wireless operator, graduating from the advanced wireless course in May 1942. Her fluent French and technical skills attracted the attention of SOE's F-Section, which offered her a post as an undercover wireless operator in occupied France. But before she could go overseas, she had to be evaluated at SOE's assessment center at Wanborough Manor near Guildford.

Her final evaluation was far from encouraging: she was scared of firearms and was not considered fit enough to do parachute training. Instead she was trained as a radio operator and sent to SOE's spy school at Beaulieu to learn how to survive in enemy territory. Her tutors noted that she was idealistic, compassionate, and selfless, but these were not qualities that were seen as particularly useful in a secret agent, who might be called upon to behave in a ruthless and dishonorable manner should the situation demand it. Her instructors at Beaulieu were less than enthusiastic, concluding that she was not suited for fieldwork.

ABOVE:
Often betrayed by German double-agents and collaborationist traitors, French Resistance networks suffered heavy losses during the occupation.

Into the lion's den
SOE chief Maurice Buckmaster (1902–92) overruled the evaluation, and sent Khan to France in mid-June 1943, where she joined the Prosper Resistance network as SOE's first female radio operator. But just ten days after her arrival in Paris a double agent betrayed the network to the Germans, and many of its members and all of its radio operators apart from Khan were arrested by the *Sicherheitsdienst* (SD; see Feature, opposite).

The posthumous citation for her George Cross made clear the risk she was taking when she decided to stay on in Paris:

She refused however to abandon what had become the principal and most dangerous post in France, although given the opportunity to return to England, because she did not wish to leave her French comrades without communications and she hoped also to rebuild her group.

Khan managed to evade capture for several months, but was eventually betrayed by a French collaborator. The SD arrested her in mid-October 1943 and she was interrogated at their Paris HQ. She proved to be much more resilient under interrogation than her English instructors would have ever believed. In postwar statements her interrogators revealed that she had "refused to give us any assistance whatsoever" and that they "could never rely on anything she said." Unfortunately, the SD had her radio, codebook, and a record of all the past messages that she had sent, and they were able to use

FEATURE **Hitler's counterspies**

Like other totalitarian dictatorships, Hitler's Third Reich depended on a large and all-powerful secret police and intelligence apparatus to control dissidents at home and opponents in the countries it had occupied. The most famous was, of course, the *Gestapo*, but it was only one of a network of organizations that were charged with rooting out and eliminating the internal and external opponents of the Nazi regime. The *Sicherheitsdienst* was established in 1931 as the *Ic-Dienst*, a small Nazi organization reporting directly to SS chief Heinrich Himmler. It became the SD in 1932, and steadily increased in power and influence as the Nazis consolidated their hold on power. The *Ausland-SD* (Overseas-SD) was the civilian counterpart of the *Abwehr* military intelligence. It was divided into six sections: Administration, Western Europe, Soviet Union and Japan, America, Eastern Europe, and Technical Matters.

them to make fake transmissions and lure seven SOE agents to their deaths.

After an unsuccessful escape attempt on November 25, 1943, she was deported to Germany, condemned to *nacht und nebel* (night and fog), an SD euphemism to describe prisoners who were to disappear without a trace. She was kept in solitary confinement and tortured for eight months but refused to give any information about her work or other SOE agents. On September 11, 1944, she was moved to Dachau concentration camp, where she was executed on the morning of September 13, 1944.

ABOVE:
Head of the SS and its counterintelligence services, Heinrich Himmler was also the man in overall charge of the Reich's infamous concentration and death camps.

NAME: **Fitzroy Maclean**

NATIONALITY: British

BIRTH: March 11, 1911
DEATH: June 15, 1996

PROFESSION: Soldier

CATEGORY: Espionage hero

ACHIEVEMENT: His undercover work changed the course of Iranian and Yugoslav history.

Although novelist Ian Fleming is supposed to have based his fictitious agent, James Bond, partly on Fitzroy Maclean, Maclean himself claimed that he had never been a spy. However, Russia's intelligence service, the NKVD, was sure he was a British agent, and he distinguished himself in undercover operations in the Near East and Yugoslavia.

If the subject of the previous entry was one of the war's most unlikely candidates to be a secret agent, Fitzroy Maclean was, according to his wife's testimony, the most likely spy who never was one. In a BBC interview soon after her husband's death, she said that while "Fitz" reveled in the idea that he had been the model for Fleming's 007, he had never been a secret agent. Although they had been involved in a secret mission, she explained: "We did once take on a spy journey on the south coast of Turkey, but Fitz's job then was simply the job of an ex-soldier, to see if there were good places where British forces could rally. So we motored all the way along in a secret Jeep, with a real spy. I loved it."

She also revealed that Maclean, like Bond, had "an eye for the ladies and was very, very brave," but unlike the fictional MI6 agent, who was always calm and collected, no matter what the situation, Maclean suffered from what we would now call post-traumatic stress disorder (PTSD). She explained: "If there was a noise in the night that woke him, he'd roll out of bed with his hands in a defensive position."

Behind the Iron Curtain

Fitzroy Maclean was the son of a Scottish nobleman, who was a major in the British army. Born in Cairo, Egypt, where his father was stationed, Maclean went to Britain's most exclusive public school, Eton College, and on to King's College, Cambridge. A career in the diplomatic service was a natural choice for a man of his background and education. He joined the Diplomatic Corps in 1933, and was posted to Paris in 1934. He found the round of social events and the undemanding work in France so boring that in 1937 he asked to be posted to the USSR, then ruled by the tyrannical Joseph Stalin (1878–1953). He remained in post in Moscow until 1939, witnessing some of the worst excesses of the Soviet regime, including the mass purges of the regime's opponents.

It was during his time in the USSR that rumors that he was a spy first began to emerge—if only in the paranoid imaginations of the agents of the NKVD. When stationed in Russia, Maclean traveled all the way from Moscow to Afghanistan and back again, visiting parts of Soviet central Asia that were normally out of bounds to foreigners, while all the time being shadowed by NKVD agents.

BELOW:
During his Moscow posting, Maclean traveled as far as Afghanistan, all the time shadowed by the NKVD, who were sure he was a British spy.

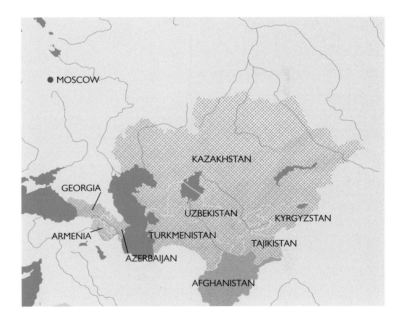

Helping Tito

Banned from enlisting because he was a career diplomat, Maclean promptly resigned, returned to Britain, and enlisted in a Scottish regiment as a private. He was one of only two men who rose from enlisted private to the rank of brigadier during the war. Amazingly, he also found time to stand for parliament and was elected as the Conservative MP for Lancaster in 1941. In 1943, after Maclean had distinguished himself in North Africa, Iraq, and Iran (see Feature, opposite), as a member of the Special Air Services (SAS) elite commando unit, Churchill sent him to Yugoslavia to find out which of the rival partisan groups was "killing the most Germans" and to "suggest means by which we could help them to kill more."

Joseph Tito (1892–1980), the leader of the Communist partisans who were fighting the Axis occupation of Yugoslavia, might not have been Churchill's first choice as his main ally in the region and as the

future prime minister and president of his country. To get the measure of the man, Churchill dispatched Maclean as his personal envoy, explaining his choice to his foreign secretary in the following memo: "Mr. Fitzroy Maclean, MP, is a man of daring character, with Foreign Office training. He is to go to Yugoslavia and work with Tito. What we want is a daring Ambassador-leader with these hardy and hunted guerrillas."

Although Maclean had witnessed the worst excesses of Communism in Stalinist Russia, and, as a member of the Scottish landed gentry, was socially worlds apart from Tito, he developed a deep sense of admiration for Tito as a man and leader of the Yugoslav struggle against fascism. He recommended that Britain should back Tito, ensuring that he would become Yugoslavia's undisputed leader in the postwar settlement. In retrospect, Maclean made an astute and fruitful recommendation; in 1948, Tito was the only leader within the Soviet sphere of influence who successfully managed to break with Stalin, establishing his own nonaligned bloc.

Maclean described his many adventures in *Eastern Approaches* (1949), published in the USA as *Escape to Adventure* (1950). He remained a firm friend of the Yugoslav people. In 1963, he was given special permission by Tito to purchase a villa on the island of Korčula (now in Croatia), at a time when foreigners were forbidden by law to own property in the Yugoslavia. In 1991, during the wars following the breakup of Yugoslavia, he and his wife delivered medical supplies to Korčula's inhabitants.

FEATURE **Kidnapping a Persian plotter**

Britain, working in concert with its allies—France, the USA, and, during the war, the USSR—was deeply involved in the internal affairs of Iran, then ruled by Reza Shah Pahlavi (1878–1944). Installed by the British in 1925, he was deposed by them in 1941, after he had declared Iranian wartime neutrality. After the shah's forced abdication, the British were worried that General Fazlollah Zahedi (ca. 1897–1963), the commander of the Isfahan Division in central Iran, was planning a military coup with German support, which, if successful, would see Iran and her extensive oil fields joining the Axis camp. The British sent Maclean to arrest Zahedi in his office in Isfahan. In full view of Zahedi troops, Maclean drove the general out of his HQ and flew him to British Palestine, where he was interned until the end of the war. Zahedi's kidnapping ended all German influence in Iran.

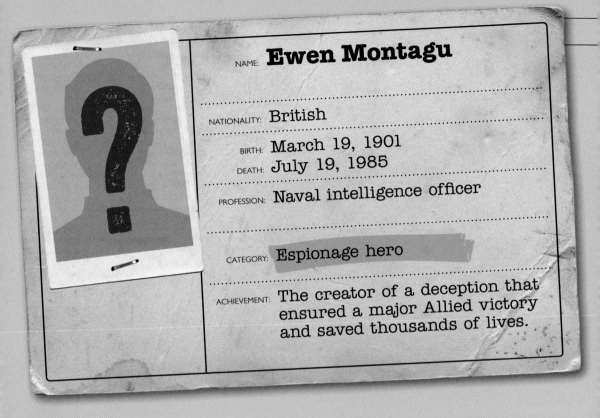

NAME: **Ewen Montagu**

NATIONALITY: British

BIRTH: March 19, 1901
DEATH: July 19, 1985

PROFESSION: Naval intelligence officer

CATEGORY: Espionage hero

ACHIEVEMENT: The creator of a deception that ensured a major Allied victory and saved thousands of lives.

Operation Mincemeat was one of the most extraordinary wartime deceptions since Odysseus' Trojan horse. But rather than a ruse to break into a besieged city, it was designed to break into a besieged continent, and to mislead the defenders as to the intended point of attack.

Subterfuge, deception, and misinformation have been part of war since remotest antiquity. It was through a trick that Odysseus ended the Greeks' ten-year stalemate in the Trojan War. But by World War II, with espionage networks, aircraft reconnaissance, codebreaking, and other intelligence techniques at the disposal of both the Allies and the Axis, the art of deception had to be much more sophisticated than building a great big wooden horse, filling it with soldiers, and leaving it on the outskirts of Berlin. As the Allies gained ground against the Axis in Europe, they planned a three-front assault on Hitler's "Fortress Europe." The British and Americans would attack from the north, from England to Normandy, and from the south across the Mediterranean Sea to Italy. This at the same time as Russia continued the battle on the Eastern Front.

Operation Torch (November 1–16, 1942), the invasion of North Africa, had assured the liberation of French North Africa (now Morocco, Algeria, and Tunisia) by Britain, the Free French, and the USA. The next logical step was an assault on southern Europe, with the most likely landing spot the island of Sicily, 100 miles (160km) from Tunisia. The problem was that, as Winston Churchill so pithily put it: "Everyone but a bloody fool would *know* that it's Sicily." And, of course, it would be impossible to hide a massive sea- and airborne invasion force once assembled. What the Allies needed to do was to trick the Germans into believing that its intended destination was not the most obvious and most accessible target, Sicily, but that they were going to attack Greece and Sardinia instead.

A near disaster

The man charged with finding a way to deceive the Germans was Captain Ewen Montagu of the British Naval Intelligence Division. His inspiration for Operation Mincemeat was the crash of a British seaplane off the Spanish coast in September 1942, which was transporting a courier who had a top-secret letter with information about Operation Torch, the planned Allied invasion of North Africa. The drowned man was recovered by the Spanish, who were supposedly neutral but were really in league with the Germans. When the courier's body was returned to the British, he still had the letter, apparently unopened. Either the Germans had not found it or they had discounted it as a deliberate plant.

After the Allied victory in North Africa, the next step was the preparation of Operation Husky, the invasion of Italy through Sicily. A few months earlier, Flight Lieutenant Charles Cholmondeley of MI5, an RAF officer who was working with Montagu on the Twenty Committee (see Feature, p. 83), had come up with the idea of

BELOW:
An Allied ship is hit during the invasion of Sicily. Operation Husky was preceded by perhaps the war's most audacious act of deception.

The snapshot of "Pam," the imaginary girlfriend of the imaginary Major Bill Martin, planted on his body as part of the personal effects of the "man who never was."

parachuting a corpse into an area where it would be found by the Germans, including a radio set with which they could feed misinformation. Together the two men modified the idea into a plan to fabricate a high-ranking military courier, carrying top-secret documents about the Allied invasion plans, whose body would wash up on the Spanish coast after an apparent plane crash.

The man who never was

The first task was to find a corpse (see Feature, opposite), that of a man of the right age and appearance, who could pass as having died by drowning. Once they had their body on ice, Cholmondeley and Montagu had to fabricate a completely believable identity for it, as well as create a series of documents that would convince the Germans that the Allied landing sites would be in Greece and Sardinia. The result was "the man who never was," who would have his brief moment of glory as "Major William Martin" of the Royal Marines.

Martin's personal effects included a snapshot of his girlfriend "Pam," a receipt for an engagement ring, various private and business letters, bills, a bus ticket, and two ticket stubs from a London playhouse. The all-important documents, several of which were written by the people concerned, included a letter from the Vice Chief of the Imperial War Staff, Lieutenant General Sir Archibald Nye (1895–1967), to General Harold Alexander (1891–1969), commander-in-chief of British forces in North Africa, as well as a letter of introduction from Martin's former commanding officer, Vice-Admiral Louis Mountbatten. Taken together, they made it plain that the Allies intended coordinated landings anywhere but Sicily.

As expected, the Spanish immediately informed Karl-Erich Kühlenthal, the most senior *Abwehr* agent in Spain, about the drowned British courier and his attaché case of documents. He arranged for them to be copied and immediately sent to Berlin. Major Martin and his documents, seemingly intact and unopened, were then returned to the British embassy. From Enigma intelligence decrypts, it soon became obvious that Hitler had been completely taken in by the deception. He withdrew troops from Italy and sent reinforcements to Greece, Sardinia, and Corsica. Even after the Allied landings in Sicily on July 9, 1943, the Germans were convinced that these were a diversionary tactic, and that they were still planning to attack elsewhere. In addition to making the invasion of Sicily much easier than it would have been, Operation Mincemeat made the Germans discount two later finds of genuine top-secret documents about military targets in Normandy after D-Day and about the invasion plans for the Netherlands.

FEATURE **Identifying the man who never was**

The man who never was, Major William Martin, was only identified in 1996 thanks to amateur historian Roger Morgan. His real name was Glyndwr Michael, a Welshman who died in London after eating rat poison. He was found in an abandoned warehouse with symptoms of acute poisoning on January 26, 1943, and died two days later in hospital. It is possible that Michael had eaten poisoned food left out for vermin rather than intentionally eaten poison to commit suicide. When the body arrived at the hospital morgue, the district coroner informed Montagu that he had found a suitable subject for him. Michael's body was kept refrigerated in the morgue until everything was in place. In April 1943, the body was placed in a specially designed air-tight container filled with dry ice to prevent decomposition, and taken to his watery grave off the Spanish coast by the British submarine *HMS Seraph*.

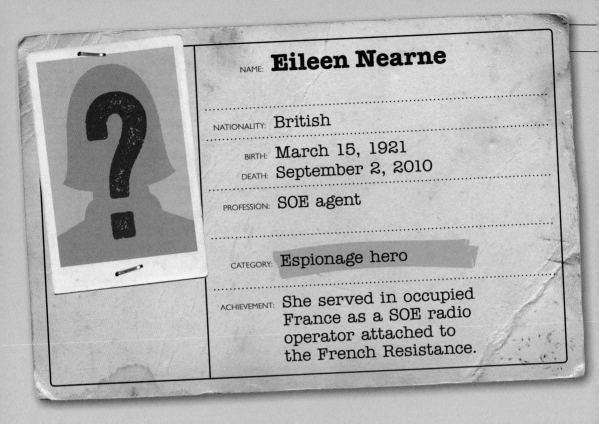

NAME: **Eileen Nearne**

NATIONALITY: British

BIRTH: March 15, 1921
DEATH: September 2, 2010

PROFESSION: SOE agent

CATEGORY: Espionage hero

ACHIEVEMENT: She served in occupied France as a SOE radio operator attached to the French Resistance.

Eileen Nearne was one of over 3,000 women who worked for SOE in various roles in Britain and in occupied Europe. Sent to France to be the radio operator for several Resistance networks, Nearne was captured and tortured by the *Gestapo*, but unlike many of her colleagues, she survived.

It would seem that SOE's female agents can be divided in two categories: those who seemed to thrive on danger and avoided capture; and those much less fortunate who fell into German hands and were tortured and ultimately executed as spies. Eileen Nearne falls somewhere between the two because, though she was arrested by the *Gestapo*, tortured, and later sent to a concentration camp, she managed to survive her ordeal to die of old age.

Nearne was also unusual in that she did not speak about her wartime activities. She did agree to take part in a BBC TV documentary about her work in France, but it was on the condition that she could wear a wig, speak in French, and use her SOE codename of "Rose." This much-decorated espionage hero remained modest and quiet to her dying day, and her achievements were rediscovered posthumously and publicized in press obituaries.

A family affair

The daughter of a Spanish mother and an English father, Eileen was the youngest of four siblings. Her sister, Jacqueline, and her brother, Francis, also worked as SOE operatives. In 1923, the family moved to France, where she learned to speak fluent French. When France fell in 1940, Eileen and Jacqueline made their way to England via Spain and Portugal to join the fight against Hitler. SOE needed agents who could pass as natives in the European countries in which they operated, and the Nearne sisters were quickly recruited. Eileen began her career as a UK-based radio operator receiving messages from SOE agents in the field, while sister Jacqueline was sent to France as a courier for the SOE Resistance networks.

An English "Rose" in France

In March 1944, it was Eileen's turn to go to France as a radio operator, with the mission to help set up a financial network to fund the French Resistance. But in July 1944, the Germans detected her transmissions and she was arrested and sent to *Gestapo* HQ in Paris. Although subjected to torture, she stuck to the story that she was an innocent French civilian tricked into sending messages by a British agent. In August 1944, she was sent to Ravensbrück concentration camp, where she refused to work, and then to a forced labor camp in Silesia, where she was mistreated and tortured. In April 1945, she escaped from the camp, and was hidden by a German priest until the area was liberated by the Americans.

LEFT:
Women SOE agents who were caught by the Germans and survived their interrogation were sent to Ravensbrück concentration camp.

NAME: **Dušan Popov**

NATIONALITY: Serbian

BIRTH: July 10, 1912

DEATH: August 10, 1981

PROFESSION: Double agent

CATEGORY: Espionage hero

ACHIEVEMENT: As a leading source of misinformation to German intelligence, he greatly assisted the Allied war effort.

Thanks to Alan Turing's cracking of Enigma encryption, the British had the upper hand in the secret war against the Axis powers. But they had just as valuable a commodity in the double agents who worked in England, and who fed their German masters a steady diet of misinformation.

There must be something very peculiar about the human psyche in that, if a person you trust implicitly tells you that something is black and not white, even though your eyes are telling you that it is white and not black, you are more likely to disbelieve the evidence of your own eyes than your human informant, especially if what he or she is telling you is something you really want to believe is true. This sums up the wartime relationship between the SD, *Gestapo*, and *Abwehr* with their agents in England and Europe, who had been turned by British intelligence to serve the Allied cause, and who relayed streams of deception and misinformation to Berlin.

Eddie Chapman (pp. 46–49) was an example of a man who first betrayed his country and then his country's enemies, and for motives that were far from noble. But he was just one of many double agents turned or run by the Double-Cross System (see Feature, p. 83). The men featured in this and the next entry, Dušan Popov and Juan Pujol García, had much more admirable motives for working as double agents for the Allies, and they played a significant role in making the D-Day landings the overwhelming successes they were.

Double double cross

Born in Serbia in 1912, when it was still a province of the Austro-Hungarian Empire, Popov grew to maturity in the newly established Yugoslavia. He was from a wealthy, well-connected family and could speak fluent German. As the Nazis were on the rise in Germany, Popov was studying for a doctorate in law at the University of Freiburg. It was then that he developed a strong and abiding hatred for Hitler and the Nazis. At the outbreak of the war, Johnny Jebsen (1917–45), who was a fellow student at Freiburg, and who had joined the *Abwehr* to avoid serving in a regular army unit, offered to recruit Popov for German intelligence. Popov got in touch with a contact at the British legation in Yugoslavia, who recruited him as a British double agent, with instructions to accept Jebsen's offer. He would be known to the British by the codename "Tricycle."

Johann JEBSEN

What Popov might not have been immediately aware of was that Jebsen was also a double agent working for the British. Jebsen was a German citizen of Danish stock, whose loathing of the Nazis was as strong as Popov's. Jebsen, however, was not as fortunate as Popov, who survived the war. He was arrested by the *Gestapo*, but not, as the British initially feared, as a double agent in the pay of the Allies, but as a criminal who had defrauded several high-ranking SS officers. He was interrogated by the *Gestapo*, who consigned him to a concentration camp. He disappeared in 1945, presumed murdered by the SS.

ABOVE:
Popov was recruited by another double agent working for the British, a former university friend of Danish origin called Johnny Jebsen, who was murdered by the SS in 1945.

Upsetting J. Edgar Hoover

The *Abwehr* set Popov up with an import–export business between Britain and neutral Portugal, which allowed him to make regular trips from London to Lisbon, where he relayed misinformation concocted for him by the Twenty Committee. In 1941, the *Abwehr* sent him to the USA to set up a network of spies, with orders to gather intelligence on specific civilian and military targets, including the defenses of the U.S. naval base at Pearl Harbor, on Oahu, Hawaii. MI6 advised the FBI of Popov's activities in the USA, and he requested a meeting with the bureau's director, J. Edgar Hoover (1895–1972).

Not only did Hoover make Popov wait before granting him an interview, he gave him a hostile reception. He shouted at the spy, "You come here from nowhere and within six weeks install yourself in a Park Avenue penthouse, chase film stars, break a serious law, and try to corrupt my officers. I'm telling you right now I won't stand for it." A stunned Popov could only reply, "I brought a serious warning indicating exactly where, when, how, and by whom your country is going to be attacked." Meaning the Japanese raid on Pearl Harbor, but Hoover was so prejudiced against the double agent that he did not act on the information himself, nor pass it on to the U.S. Navy.

Fooling Hitler

Although the Allies had already deceived the Germans over their invasion plans for Sicily (see Ewen Montagu, pp. 74–77), they do not seem to have learned from past mistakes. In March 1944, preparations were well advanced for the D-Day landings scheduled for the month of June. The most obvious place for the Allies to choose was the Pas de Calais, a mere 20.6 miles (33km) across the Channel from the Kent coast, but they had opted for the more distant but less-heavily-fortified beaches of Normandy.

BELOW:
Although Popov warned
Hoover that the Japanese
were interested in Pearl
Harbor's defenses, the U.S.
was completely unprepared
for the December 7 raid.

Popov was one of several double agents whose misinformation was crucial to the success of Operation Fortitude (see Feature, p. 87), a massive deception the Allies had set up to convince Hitler that their intended target was Calais. Jebsen's arrest by the *Gestapo* temporarily put the whole operation on hold, and led to Popov's temporary decommissioning, because Jebsen knew about Britain's network of double agents. But thanks to Enigma decrypts, the Allies realized that Jebsen had not betrayed any secrets during interrogation, and Fortitude and Popov were reactivated, leading to Hitler to reinforce the Pas de Calais, greatly easing the Allied landings in Normandy.

FEATURE | **Bureau for misinformation**

One is almost tempted to feel sorry for wartime German intelligence, such was its ineptitude. Perhaps it is something to do with the fascist mindset that sees the world in primary colors rather than the more nuanced reality of shades merging into one another. According to wartime records, it seems that all but one of the agents the Germans sent to Britain were captured and turned by section B1(a) of MI5, and then used against their former masters by the Twenty Committee, which ran the Double-Cross System, providing them with a constant stream of misinformation. The committee, which included Ewen Montagu, was overseen not by a military man, but tellingly by an academic and author, John Cecil Masterman (1891–1977). Its success proved once again that in order to succeed, rather than blind devotion to an ideology, espionage needs imagination and freedom of thought.

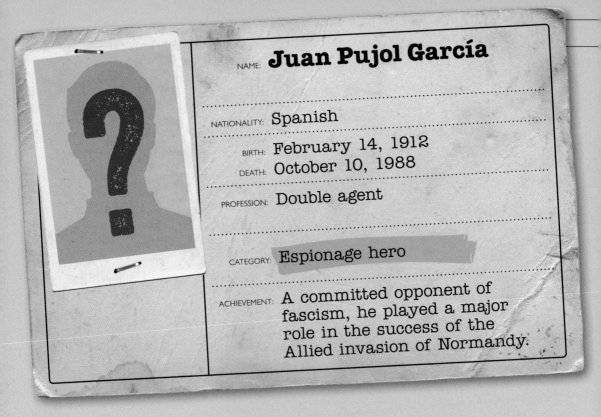

NAME:	**Juan Pujol García**
NATIONALITY:	Spanish
BIRTH:	February 14, 1912
DEATH:	October 10, 1988
PROFESSION:	Double agent
CATEGORY:	Espionage hero
ACHIEVEMENT:	A committed opponent of fascism, he played a major role in the success of the Allied invasion of Normandy.

Juan Pujol García was initially rejected by British intelligence. Undeterred, he offered his services to the Germans, but with the intention of acting as a freelance double agent with an extensive but totally bogus network of agents in Britain. After the Allies recognized his value, he played a key role in Operation Fortitude.

If you want to deceive someone, the easiest way is to try to make them believe something they half believe (or fear) already. When Ewen Montagu created "the man who never was," he was counting on Hitler's paranoia to make him think that the British and Americans were attempting a double-bluff. Sicily was the most likely landing site, and he was sure that they wanted him to believe they would go there rather than Greece and Sardinia. In the spring of 1944, the Allies had to persuade Hitler of the exact opposite—that they would land in the Pas de Calais rather than Normandy.

In order to persuade Hitler, his generals, and his intelligence services, the Allies devised the largest deception ever mounted, Operation Fortitude (see Feature, p. 87). A key element of the plan was to

ABOVE:
American troops landing in Vichy-controlled French Algeria in 1942—one of several operations obscured by webs of deceit spun with planted documents and fake reports.

feed a constant stream of misinformation to German intelligence through the network of double agents controlled by the Double-Cross System: men like Dušan Popov and, the subject of this entry, Juan Pujol García.

A curse on both your houses

Pujol was the third son of a wealthy industrialist from Catalonia, then, as now, a fiercely independent province, whose leftwing sympathies made it side with Spain's Second Republic (1931–39) against General Francisco Franco's (1892–1975) fascists during the Spanish Civil War (1936–39). Although by virtue of his nationality Pujol should have supported the republic, and by virtue of his class, Franco and his Catholic fascists, having witnessed the excesses of both sides during the Civil War, he developed an equal dislike for the extremes of both left and right. The Communists and Anarcho-syndicalists had seized the family business and mistreated his mother and sister, and the fascists had persecuted him for his monarchist views. His antipathy thus extended to their respective backers, fascist Germany and Italy, and Communist Russia.

The freelance spy

When war broke out, the fascist dictatorships in Spain and Portugal remained ostensibly neutral but in reality sided with the Axis. Pujol, having failed to interest the British as a potential spy, decided to start a one-man intelligence war against the Axis. That a Spanish citizen not only supported the Nazis but wished to work for them as a spy would not have come as a surprise to the German backers of General Franco. With a fake background as a Spanish diplomat and fanatical Nazi, Pujol offered his services to German intelligence, who enthusiastically welcomed him into its ranks. They trained and equipped him, and gave him £600 ($12,000 in 2015) to begin recruiting a network of agents in Britain.

But instead of moving to England, Pujol went to Lisbon, from where he pretended to fulfill his mission of recruiting a network of British agents, sending reports that seemed to originate in London. To make his reports credible, he used information gleaned from a travel guide to the UK, library books and magazines, and movie theater newsreels. Although he made several errors and never understood Britain's pre-decimal currency, he succeeded in fooling his German paymasters, and for a while the British, who had been alerted to the existence of a new spy networks thanks to Enigma decrypts. By the beginning of 1942, having got the attention of both the British and Americans, Pujol offered them his services once more.

"I want to be alone"

This time British were not slow in realizing what a valuable asset Pujol could be. In April 1942, he was moved to England and integrated into the Twenty Committee's Double-Cross System. With typical British humor, Pujol was given the codename "Garbo," after the actress Greta Garbo (1905–90), who famously said, "I want to be alone." By the end of the war, Pujol's fictional network of spies had grown to 27 agents, which provided so much intelligence to Berlin that the Germans no longer felt the need to establish further spy networks in Britain.

At first, the bogus reports were sent by airmail to Lisbon, which allowed him to pass on genuine information, timing it to arrive just after it might have been useful. A report on troop movements connected to Operation Torch

FEATURE **The better to deceive**

The scale of Operation Fortitude dwarfed any campaign of deceit attempted during World War II (and perhaps during any war), because of the scale of what had to be hidden: the Operation Overlord invasion force made up of 1,200 aircraft, 5,000 ships and landing craft, and 160,000 troops. Fortitude was divided into two parts: an invasion of Norway from Scotland, and one of the Pas de Calais from the south coast of England. Fortitude consisted of five different kinds of "special means": dummy military infrastructure and equipment; leaks to third parties through diplomatic channels; dummy wireless traffic; the creation of FUSAG, a bogus U.S. command under General George S. Patton (1885–1945); and the deployment of all the German double agents, real and imagined, controlled by the Twenty Committee and the Double-Cross System, notably, agents "Tricycle," "Garbo," and "Brutus," aka Dušan Popov, Juan Pujol García, and Roman Czerniawski (1910–85).

earned him a commendation, though the letter arrived after the invasion of North Africa. When the Germans equipped him with a radio, his reports, which were encoded in Madrid with an Enigma machine for retransmission to Berlin, assisted in the breaking of Enigma encryption.

Pujol's greatest contribution to the war effort was to come during the build-up to the D-Day landings, when he played a key role in Operation Fortitude (see Feature, above). He sent hundreds of messages to the German High Command, warning them that the Normandy landings were a diversionary tactic, and that the main attack would come at the Pas de Calais. His information was so trusted that for weeks after D-Day, German divisions were held back from the main theater of operations, enabling the Allies to establish a secure bridgehead in France.

ABOVE:

In addition to fake intelligence reports and dummy radio chatter, Operation Fortitude used inflatable tanks to hide the location of real military assets and their intended landing sites.

NAME: **Odette Sansom**

NATIONALITY: French

BIRTH: April 28, 1912
DEATH: March 13, 1995

PROFESSION: SOE agent

CATEGORY: Espionage hero

ACHIEVEMENT: A hero of SOE and the French Resistance, she survived capture, torture, and deportation to Germany.

Although Odette Sansom's career in SOE was tragically short, she demonstrated extraordinary resilience and heroism when captured and tortured by German counterintelligence. Condemned to deportation and death in a concentration camp, she was saved by claiming to be related by marriage to Prime Minister Winston Churchill.

After two entries that demonstrated the complete ineptitude of German intelligence—how their networks of spies in Britain were either imaginary or subverted by the British, and how their most secret communications were read by the Allies—we need a reminder that World War II espionage was not some kind of big adventure played by overgrown schoolboys. German counterintelligence—the SD and the *Gestapo*— employed both technological and tried-and-tested means to capture Allied agents. These included radio interception and surveillance, and threats, torture, and bribery, all of which feature in the story of Odette Sansom, the only woman ever to have received the George Cross, the UK's highest award for civilian gallantry, while she was still alive (the other awards made to female SOE agents were all posthumous).

An accidental spy

Sansom was born in France, the daughter of a World War I hero who died in 1918. At the age of 14, she moved to the French resort of Boulogne-sur-Mer in the Pas de Calais, where she met and married her husband, British hotelier Roy Sansom. In 1931, the couple had a daughter and moved back to England, where they had another two daughters. At the outbreak of war, her husband enlisted and Sansom and her daughters moved to the relative safety of the west of England. In 1942, the BBC broadcast an appeal on behalf of the Admiralty for photographs of the French coast for intelligence purposes. Sansom sent snaps of her adolescence in Boulogne but misaddressed them to the War Ministry, where they came to the attention of SOE's F-Section.

Homeward bound

Sansom was a good candidate for intelligence work, though her SOE instructors warned that she was "impulsive and hasty in her judgments," and that "her main weakness is a complete unwillingness to admit that she could ever be wrong." In November 1942, SOE sent her to the French Riviera, with orders to make her way to Auxerre in central France. She met up with Peter Churchill (1909–72), the head of the "Spindle" network in Cannes, but was unable to proceed to Auxerre as planned.

She remained with Churchill, working for Spindle and narrowly avoiding capture several times. In March 1943, the *Abwehr* succeeded in infiltrating Spindle, and Sansom and Churchill were arrested. She was taken to the SD's headquarters, where she was tortured. What saved both their lives was her claim that she was married to Peter Churchill and that he was related to Prime Minister Winston Churchill. As a valuable prisoner, he was taken to Berlin, but she was sent for liquidation to Germany with other SOE agents, including Andrée Borrel (pp. 128–131). Her supposed relationship to the British premier again saved her life, as the commandant of Ravensbrück concentration camp kept her alive to use her as a bargaining chip with the approaching Allies.

NAME: **Leonard Siffleet**

NATIONALITY: Australian

BIRTH: January 14, 1916

DEATH: October 24, 1943

PROFESSION: Soldier

CATEGORY: Espionage hero

ACHIEVEMENT: Operated behind enemy lines to gather intelligence on Japanese troop movements.

Leonard Siffleet was one of many Australians and New Zealanders who served in Australia's Services Reconnaissance Department in the Asia-Pacific theater, operating behind enemy lines in Indonesia and Papua New Guinea. Captured, he was exposed to the full brutality of the Japanese military and beheaded.

This entry looks at the other great theater of operations during World War II, the Asia-Pacific, where the Allies opposed the forces of the Empire of Japan. Imperial Japan was unlike its Axis allies, Germany and Italy, in that it was not a fascist one-party state headed by a self-appointed dictator but nominally a constitutional monarchy with an elected parliament, the Diet, established on the British model by the Meiji Constitution of 1890. However, the inexorable rise of militarism and ultra-nationalism during the 1930s snuffed out Japan's brief democratic experiment and drove it to invade the Republic of China in 1937 and declare a suicidal war of expansion against Britain, the Netherlands, and the United States in 1941.

The extraordinary speed of Japanese expansion after the surprise attack on Pearl Harbor meant that by 1942 Australia had become the Allied front line in Asia-Pacific. Not only was Australia woefully unprepared militarily for the storm that was heading its way, it had a limited intelligence capacity. The former shortcoming was resolved by the creation of the Second Australian Imperial Force (AIF) and the latter, in March 1942, by the formation of the Allied Intelligence Bureau (AIB), an agency bringing together British, U.S., Dutch, and Australian intelligence personnel in the region.

The boy from Gunnedah

Born in Gunnedah, a small agricultural community in New South Wales, the young Siffleet wanted to join the NSW police force but failed to pass the physical because of poor eyesight. In 1940, before the Japanese entry into the war, he was drafted in the country's only fighting force, the Australian militia, but was discharged three months later. In September 1941, he volunteered for the AIF and was posted to the signals corps. Having completed a course as a specialist radio operator at the Melbourne Technical College, he volunteered for special operations behind enemy lines.

ABOVE:
After the raid on Pearl Harbor and the capture of Singapore, the Japanese posed a significant threat to Australia, which in 1941 had very limited intelligence capabilities.

Siffleet was posted to Services Reconnaissance Department (SRD), also know as Special Operations Australia (SOA), which was modeled on the British SOE. He was assigned as a radio operator to Z Special Unit, a reconnaissance and sabotage special forces organization that operated in the Asia-Pacific theater. During the war, Z Special Unit would carry out 81 intelligence and sabotage missions, including two successful attacks on shipping in the harbor of Japanese-occupied Singapore.

RIGHT:
Japanese recruits in training in 1942. Japan's military conquests quickly placed Australia under direct threat.

In May 1943, Siffleet was promoted to the rank of sergeant and reassigned to SRD's M Special Unit, an organization whose brief was to gather intelligence on Japanese shipping and troop movements from behind enemy lines. Siffleet's first mission with M Special Unit was the surveillance of enemy traffic in and around Hollandia in the Dutch East Indies (now Jayapura City, Papua, Indonesia). Siffleet's four-man group, codenamed "Whiting," consisted of a Dutch sergeant and two privates from the Indonesian island of Ambon. They were to work with another SRD group codenamed "Locust."

Execution in Aitape

In mid-September, two members of Siffleet's unit, his Dutch sergeant and one of the Ambonese privates, who had gone on reconnaissance, were ambushed by hostile Papuans. The sergeant was killed but the private managed to escape and rejoin Whiting. Siffleet then radioed a warning to Locust about hostile locals and Japanese activity in the area and indicated that he was about to burn his codebooks and bury his radio in preparation for making his way back across the border into Papua New Guinea (PNG). Nothing more was heard from the three men, and their fate remained unknown until the end of the war.

Some time in October, Siffleet and his two Ambonese companions were ambushed by 100 hostile Papua New Guineans in the vicinity of the small town of Aitape. All three men were captured and handed over to the Japanese. Siffleet was interrogated and tortured in nearby Malol but refused to talk. He and his companions were sent to Aitape, where they were imprisoned for several weeks.

On the afternoon of October 24, 1943, the Japanese took Siffleet and his two companions to Aitape beach. They were bound and blindfolded and made to kneel before an audience of locals and Japanese soldiers. A sentence of death by beheading had been handed down by the regional commander, Vice-Admiral Michiaki Kamada (1890–1947) of the Imperial Japanese Navy. The Japanese officer who executed the sentence, Yasuno Chikao, was photographed as he was about to strike the fatal blow. The snapshot was discovered on the body of a dead Japanese officer by American troops six months later.

The photograph, which is thought to be the only extant depiction of the execution of a Western prisoner by the Japanese, was published by the Australian press and by *Life* magazine in the USA, becoming one of the iconic images of the Pacific conflict. Initially, the man in the photo was misidentified as Australian pilot William Newton (1919–43), who had been beheaded by the Japanese after being shot down in March 1943. The misidentification was corrected in 1945. Siffleet's name is recorded on the Commonwealth War memorial in Lae, PNG, and in 2015 a memorial garden was dedicated to his memory in Aitape.

RIGHT:
Siffleet was a member of the SRD, which was responsible for reporting on Japanese troop movements in the occupied Dutch East Indies and Papua New Guinea.

FEATURE **Japan's *Gestapo***

The *Kempeitai* (military police corps), founded in 1881 during the Meiji Period (1868–1912), exercised a large number of functions within Japan and its prewar colonies of Taiwan and Korea, as well as in the occupied territories during the Pacific War. In addition to acting as the military police force for the Imperial Japanese Army and Navy, it provided manpower for the Interior and Justice ministries in Japan, and fulfilled the functions of a secret police and counter-espionage organization at home and overseas. Once Japan joined the Axis in 1940, the *Kempeitai* established links with the German *Abwehr* and Italian *Servizio Informazioni Militari*, and with the SS and its two intelligence organizations, the SD and *Gestapo*. According to U.S. reports, the *Kempeitai* employed 36,000 regular officers and many more auxiliaries in Japan's colonies and the occupied territories. The organization's duties included homeland security, counterintelligence and counterpropaganda, wartime requisitioning and rationing, and labor recruitment.

Richard Sorge

NAME:	**Richard Sorge**
NATIONALITY:	German and Russian
BIRTH:	October 4, 1895
DEATH:	November 7, 1944
PROFESSION:	Military intelligence officer
CATEGORY:	Espionage hero
ACHIEVEMENT:	By informing Stalin that Japan was not planning to attack Russia, he hastened Hitler's defeat.

Richard Sorge's five decades on Earth spanned two world wars and a career as a master spy in Europe and East Asia. Both Russian and German by birth, he pledged his allegiance to Stalin's Soviet Union at the moment of her greatest peril. Arrested, he was disowned by Stalin and only rehabilitated by his successor.

To John Le Carré (b. 1931), Richard Sorge was "the spy to end spies"; to Ian Fleming, "the most formidable spy in history"; and to Tom Clancy (1947–2013), "the best spy of all time." Such high praise does not come lightly from the pens of three of the world's most successful writers of espionage fiction. But even when compared to the other men and women featured in this book, who were noted for their heroism or whose deeds made a significant contribution to the Allied cause—and in many cases, for both—Sorge stands out as a one-off. The influence he had on the outcome of the war and the subsequent history of humanity is arguably without parallel.

Of course, there is one glaring inconsistency that jars with the above picture of unrivaled brilliance: Sorge was arrested, confessed to being a spy under torture, and was executed. By rights, like a real-life James Bond, he should have bested all his enemies, retired from the fray a much-fêted and decorated hero, and died in bed, possibly with a partner many years younger than himself. Even recognition for his achievements had to wait for the death of Joseph Stalin and the accession of his successor, Nikita Khrushchev (1894–1971), who after seeing the 1961 French movie *Qui êtes-vous, Monsieur Sorge?* (*Who Are You, Mr. Sorge?*), asked his intelligence chief for a full report on the Sorge affair. Only then, some two decades after his execution, was Sorge finally recognized by the USSR with the award of its highest decoration: the Gold Star of a Hero of the Soviet Union.

Divided loyalties

Sorge was born in Baku (formerly part of the Russian Empire and Soviet Union, now the capital of Azerbaijan) to a Russian mother and a German father, who had come to work in the Caucasus oil fields. Although we are now used to transcontinental marriages, in pre-World War I Europe, Sorge's international parentage and exotic birthplace would have set him apart from his more conventional peers when he returned to Germany as boy.

BELOW:
The Berlin headquarters of the Communist Party. After Germany's defeat in 1918, there was a very real chance that the country would go the way of Soviet Russia.

In 1914, the 19-year old Sorge enlisted in the German army, serving on the Western Front. He was badly wounded in 1916 and invalided out of the armed forces. The experience left him with a deep and abiding dislike of war. While convalescing, he studied Karl Marx (1818–83) and became a Communist. He spent the rest of the war studying political science, earning his doctorate in 1919. He joined the German Communist Party, and as early as 1920 was involved in espionage activities in Germany while working as a newspaper journalist. In 1924, he moved to Russia, where he worked for the intelligence-gathering arm of the Comintern. In 1929, he was recruited as an agent by the GRU (see Feature, p. 97), the organization he would serve until his death.

Establishing cover

After a brief mission to the UK to report on the British labor and Communist movements, Sorge returned to Germany in 1929, where the GRU instructed him to join the Nazi Party and obtain a job with a German newspaper. Equipped with his new Nazi and journalistic credentials, he went to China, where he contacted members of the Chinese Communist Party and kept Moscow informed about the undeclared war between Republican China and Imperial Japan. In 1933, in preparation for his next mission, this time to Japan, Sorge returned to Germany, where he posed as a committed Nazi, making contacts in the higher echelons of the party, and obtained commissions from several German newspapers to act as their correspondent in Japan. As far as anyone was concerned, Sorge was an enthusiastic Nazi with impeccable credentials.

Changing history

It would not be an exaggeration to say that Sorge changed the history of the world after 1941. Nazi Germany and Stalinist Russia had signed a nonaggression pact in 1939, but by 1941 it was clear that Hitler was planning to invade Russia. What Stalin most feared was a simultaneous attack by Germany from the west and Japan from the east. Sorge, who had entrées in German and Japanese diplomatic circles in Tokyo, and a network of Japanese and foreign agents, including Hotsumi Ozaki (pp. 156–157), was ideally placed to tell Stalin what he needed to know.

ABOVE:
In order to be above suspicion when spying for the Soviet Union in Tokyo, Sorge first went back to Berlin, where he pretended to be an enthusiastic Nazi supporter.

Stalin, however, distrusted the hard-drinking German-born Sorge, who had a taste for high capitalist living. When Sorge warned that Operation Barbarossa—Hitler's invasion of Russia—would start on June 20 or 22, Stalin dismissed the information out of hand, much to his country's cost as German Panzers rolled in, crushing all opposition. But Stalin did believe the second piece of information Sorge sent in September: that Japan would not

attack Russia until a German victory seemed assured. This allowed Stalin to move reinforcements from the east, which ultimately led to the reversal of German fortunes in the winter of 1941.

In October, the *Kempeitai*, which had been listening in to Sorge's coded transmissions, finally moved to arrest him. At first, there was some confusion as to which country he might be spying for: Germany or Russia. In the end, both countries disowned him, the *Abwehr* correctly, as he had never been a double agent. Tortured, Sorge confessed to being a Soviet spy. He was executed on November 7, 1944, after the GRU had refused three times to acknowledge him as one of their own and to save him by trading him for a Japanese agent.

ABOVE:
German troops crossing into Soviet territory in June 1941. Hitler's only chance of success in Russia depended on a Japanese attack on the Soviet Union from the east.

FEATURE **From Russia with spies**

The GRU, or the Main Intelligence Directorate of the General Staff of the Armed Forces of the Russian Federation (formerly of the Soviet Union), is unusual among wartime intelligence agencies in that it still exists, unlike its Allied counterparts the OSS and the SOE, which were quickly disbanded at the end of hostilities. Although the Soviet KGB is far better known in the West, the GRU employed far more overseas agents, as well as commanding its own battalions of *Spetsnaz* (special operations troops). Originally known as the Registration Directorate, or RU, the GRU was established by the creator of the Red Army, Leon Trotsky (1879–1940), who fell out with Stalin, went into exile, and was murdered on the dictator's orders. After several reorganizations during the mid-1920s to weaken Trotsky's influence, the GRU became independent of the Red Army, reporting directly to the Politburo on all matters of foreign political and military intelligence.

NAME: **Violette Szabo**

NATIONALITY: French and British

BIRTH: June 26, 1921
DEATH: February 5, 1945

PROFESSION: SOE agent

CATEGORY: Espionage hero

ACHIEVEMENT: An inspirational espionage hero, she was steadfast to the end, maintaining the morale of fellow prisoners.

When her husband was killed fighting the Germans, Violette Szabo decided that the best way to honor his memory, and fight for what she believed in, was to volunteer to work undercover in France as an SOE agent. Captured, tortured, and murdered, she represents the most noble, heroic, and selfless face of espionage.

Not every spy can be a Richard Sorge (see previous entry), who changed the course of world history. Most wartime agents had much more modest careers, sometimes amounting to no more than one or two missions before they were arrested, tortured, and imprisoned or executed. But looking at many of the entries featured in this section, the true measure of an espionage hero is not accounted for solely by the number of tanks, ships, and planes destroyed, or the number of Allied lives saved and enemy lives taken, but in the courage that an individual displayed in their darkest hours, when there was no hope of rescue, and the only deliverance would come from the executioner's bullet.

Like Noor-un-Nisa Inayat Khan (pp. 66–69) and Leonard Siffleet (pp. 90–93), Violette Szabo's career as a spy was all too brief. Her capture is evidence that the Germans, though prone to falling for huge deceptions, such as Operations Mincemeat and Fortitude, were often frighteningly efficient in the theory and practice of counterintelligence, including infiltrating SOE–Resistance networks and luring agents to their deaths with fake transmissions sent via captured SOE radios. It was only after the war, when SOE's Vera Atkins (1908–2000; see Feature, p. 100) traveled across Europe to discover the fate of many missing agents, that the scale of SOE losses was finally known.

Black widow

Szabo had good reason to loathe the Nazis. Not only had they waged war on both countries she called home—Britain through her father and France through her mother—but they had deprived her of the man she loved and the father of her only daughter, Tania. The 19-year-old Violette met a French officer of Hungarian descent, Etienne Szabo, at the Bastille Day celebrations in London on July 14, 1940. Five weeks later they married. In a period when no one knew whether they would be alive the following day, let alone in a year's time, such matrimonial haste was not unusual.

ABOVE:
After the fall of France, members of the French armed forces escaped to England, where General de Gaulle established the headquarters of the Free French.

The couple enjoyed a week's honeymoon before Etienne was shipped off to Africa, where he took part in several campaigns against Vichy France forces. Violette, keen to support the war effort, enlisted in the Auxiliary Territorial Service (ATS), training as an anti-aircraft gunner, but when she realized that she was pregnant, she resigned from the ATS and went to London to have her baby. On June 8, 1942, she gave birth to her and Etienne's only child. Etienne was never to see his daughter; he was killed during the Second Battle of El Alamein on October 24, 1942.

ABOVE:

The remains of Rouen cathedral in June 1944. Two months earlier, Szabo had traveled to the city on her first mission for F-Section.

One-woman war

A distraught Violette accepted an offer to join SOE as an undercover agent in France, seeing it as the best way she could defeat the enemy that had taken her beloved Etienne. Her fluency in French and her ATS training made her an attractive recruit for SOE's F-Section. Her evaluation said that she was "plucky and persistent," but carried a disappointing grade "D"—only just good enough to get her onto the next stage of paramilitary and commando training. Her instructors found her a puzzle: she was completely dedicated and willing, but at the same time they thought she was "too fatalistic" and temperamentally unsuited for undercover work.

F-Section chief Maurice Buckmaster and his assistant Vera Atkins, as they had done before with several other less-than-ideal candidates, decided that the need for agents outweighed the risk of using her. Violette's first assignment was to discover the state of the "Salesman" network in Rouen. After reporting that it had been fatally compromised by the *Gestapo*, she was flown back to London. Her second mission was to central France, where SOE was trying to create the "Salesman II" network, to assist Allied forces that had already landed in Normandy. A car carrying Szabo and three Resistance fighters was stopped at a German checkpoint. A firefight ensued and Szabo was captured. She was interrogated by the SD in Limoges and later tortured by the *Gestapo* in Paris.

FEATURE | **The formidable Vera**

Although she had no prior intelligence training and had joined SOE as a secretary, Romanian-born Vera Atkins rose to be F-Section chief Maurice Buckmaster's personal assistant. She was in charge of the recruitment, training, and deployment of agents, with special responsibility for the 37 female agents sent to the various SOE–Resistance networks. As mentioned in the entry on Inayat Khan, although a report had been made about her capture, Buckmaster and Atkins continued to treat Khan's transmissions as genuine, leading to the loss of at least seven other agents. There is no question that either was a double agent, but they were criticized for failing to spot evidence that the SD had captured SOE radio operators and were using their transmitters. In 1945–46, Atkins traveled across Europe in order to discover the fate of the missing agents and to testify at the trials of their murderers.

The disappeared

As the Allies closed in on Paris, the SS decided to move their more valuable prisoners to Germany. After a hellish eight-day journey by train and truck, during which Szabo was permanently shackled to fellow SOE agent Denise Bloch (1916–45), the exhausted, half-starved female prisoners arrived at Ravensbrück concentration camp. The mistreatment continued through the fall and winter of 1944. The women were made to do forced labor outdoors wearing only their summer clothes; they lived in unheated barracks; and they were given starvation rations. Throughout her ordeal, Szabo remained defiant and was sure that they would be liberated by the advancing Allies. She encouraged her fellow prisoners to remain optimistic and continually made plans to escape.

With the Allies advancing on Ravensbrück, and the end of the war a few months away, the SS decided to liquidate all captive SOE agents before they could be liberated. At the end of January 1945, three SOE agents, including Szabo and Bloch, were shot in the back of the head and their bodies immediately cremated. Szabo was one of three F-Section female agents to be awarded Britain's highest decoration, the George Cross, for her wartime service, for which she also received the *Croix de Guerre* and the *Médaille de la Resistance*.

BELOW:
Hitler and Himmler inspect an SS unit in Klagenfurt, Germany, in 1938. The SS was notorious for its brutality toward prisoners in German-occupied territories.

NAME: **Leopold Trepper**

NATIONALITY: Polish and Russian

BIRTH: February 23, 1904
DEATH: January 19, 1982

PROFESSION: GRU agent

CATEGORY: Espionage hero

ACHIEVEMENT: He established the "Red Orchestra," the largest Soviet intelligence networks in occupied Europe.

A committed Communist, Leopold Trepper had a checkered career as a spy before and during the war. The organizer of the Red Orchestra, he was arrested and briefly worked for the Germans, before absconding and going underground in Paris. After the war, instead of rewarding him, the Russians imprisoned him for ten years.

In the murky world of World War II espionage, it is sometimes difficult to differentiate the good guys from the bad guys, especially if one's perspective is colored by subsequent historical events, such as the 50-year Cold War (1948–91) between the liberal-democratic capitalist West and the Communist East. This might explain why, although we may respect men such as

Richard Sorge (pp. 94–97) and the subject of the current entry, we find it much easier to express our admiration and respect for less ambiguous espionage heroes such as Violette Szabo (see previous entry) and Noor-un-Nisa Inayat Khan (pp. 66–69), who, while they may not have achieved as much in practical terms for the Allied war effort, were morally unimpeachable.

Both Sorge and Trepper had difficult relationships with their commander-in-chief, Soviet dictator Joseph Stalin—despite, or maybe because, he owed his political and military survival to the information they had provided. Mother Russia went as far as denying all knowledge of Sorge, and when Trepper returned to his adoptive homeland after the war, far from being rewarded and hailed as a Soviet hero, he spent ten years in jail. Stalin seems to have had a strong dislike for both men, but the offence was compounded in Trepper's case by his being a Jew, an active Zionist, and a Pole by birth—each attribute alone would have been enough to have him marked for persecution by the NKVD.

In spite of his less-than-friendly postwar treatment by the Soviet regime, he remained a committed Communist to the last. In his autobiography, *The Great Game* (1975), he wrote, "I do not regret the commitment of my youth, I do not regret the paths I have taken," stressing the difference between the ideology he had dedicated his life to and the state he had served with distinction and which had betrayed and persecuted him.

ABOVE:
Although he had helped save Soviet dictator Joseph Stalin, Trepper was not rewarded after the war but arrested by the NKVD, interrogated, and imprisoned.

A young Zionist-Communist

Trepper had a difficult childhood as the son of a Jewish Polish family and developed an early awareness of how his Jewish identity set him apart from Poland's Catholic majority. His father died when Trepper was only 12 years old, leaving his mother struggling to pay for his education. Although he graduated from high school and had ambitions to go to university to study history and literature, he did not have the funds to continue studying, and instead became a miner in the Upper Silesian coal fields. An early convert to Soviet-style Communism, the 19-year-old Trepper organized an illegal strike, which landed him in prison for eight months.

FEATURE | **Defending Mother Russia**

Stalinist Russia, like Nazi Germany, was a one-party state, governed by a self-appointed dictator. Joseph Stalin, like Hitler, depended on an increasingly oppressive state security apparatus to eliminate domestic rivals, crush internal dissent, and gather information about foreign enemies. In addition to its military intelligence service, the GRU, the Soviet state established the People's Commissariat for Internal Affairs, the NKVD, which began as an internal security organization that was also in charge of the traffic and border police forces and the fire service. During the Stalinist purges (1936–38), the NKVD became increasingly centralized and acted as the main security arm of the ruling Communist Party, while the GRU served the same function within the Red Army. Tasked with protecting the integrity and stability of the Soviet Union, the NKVD developed a significant overseas capability (later inherited by the KGB), overseeing espionage, political assassinations of Russian exiles, and the control of foreign Communist movements.

Upon his release, Trepper decided to fight for another ideal, Zionism, the Jewish movement for aliyah, or return to the land of Israel. He emigrated to the British mandate of Palestine but was expelled for anti-British activities in 1929. For the next three years he lived in France, where he was a member of a banned Communist organization, until he was again forced to flee in order to avoid arrest by French security services.

The red conductor

Trepper escaped to the only country in Europe that would give him asylum and employment, the Soviet Union. He was quickly recruited by the NKVD (see Feature, above), which sent him back to Western Europe to set up a spy network. Codenamed *Die Rote Kapelle*, the Red Orchestra, by German counterintelligence, the network was headquartered in Belgium and ran agents in Germany, France, the Netherlands, and Switzerland. Trepper's "orchestra" was the largest Soviet spy ring in occupied Europe, and probably second in importance, in the context of the impact it had on the war, only to Richard Sorge's Japanese operation.

Like Sorge, Trepper alerted Moscow of eastward German troop movements and warned Stalin that Hitler was about to invade, but again the dictator ignored the information. In 1941 the *Abwehr* tracked the group's Brussels transmitter, and arrested and tortured Red Orchestra agents, leading to the dismantling of the entire network. Trepper managed to escape to Paris, where he went to ground, until he, too, was arrested in November 1942.

Down but not out in Paris

Trepper was faced with a difficult choice. He was so valuable a prize that the Germans wanted him as a double agent. British author Patrick Marnham claimed that to save himself Trepper betrayed a Soviet agent in Paris and also Resistance leader Jean Moulin. At the same time,

however, he managed to let the NKVD know that he had been compromised and was acting under duress.

In September 1943, this inveterate survivor escaped his German captors and hid with the Communist Underground in Paris until the city's liberation on August 19, 1944. It is unclear why Trepper was imprisoned upon his return to the Soviet Union. It might have been for his presumed act of betrayal in 1942, or as part of the many purges and persecutions that marked Stalin's rule. Trepper was released after the dictator's death, and returned to Poland, where he remained until 1974, when he was finally allowed to emigrate to the State of Israel, where he died in 1982.

ABOVE:
U.S. infantry march down the Champs Élysées in August 1944. The liberation of Paris allowed Trepper to emerge from hiding, only to be arrested upon arrival back in the USSR.

NAME: Nancy Wake

NATIONALITY: New Zealander and Australian

BIRTH: August 30, 1912

DEATH: August 7, 2011

PROFESSION: SOE agent

CATEGORY: Espionage hero

ACHIEVEMENT: One of the most effective wartime SOE agents, she created a formidable Resistance army.

Nicknamed "the White Mouse" by the *Gestapo* because of their inability to capture her, Nancy Wake began the war helping Jews and British servicemen escape from German-occupied and Vichy France. During the buildup to D-Day, she organized and led one of the most formidable Resistance groups in central France.

A great many of the histories covered in this section have decidely unhappy conclusions, so much so that they seem to encourage the kind of pessimistic fatalism that afflicted Odette Sansom (pp. 88–89)—even with the omission of the most harrowing details of the torture that captured operatives were subjected to. But in the midst of all these examples of heroic sacrifice, we find an outspoken, unstoppable Antipodean so dynamic and resilient that she easily tilts the scales the other way, restoring our faith that good can sometimes thumb its nose at evil, challenge it to do its worse, and come out victorious.

If Ian Fleming had not been a misogynist and had ever created a female MI6 agent, he would have probably modeled her on Nancy Wake. Absolutely fearless, calm under pressure, and also lucky, she finished the war as the most decorated Allied servicewoman, garnering 12 of the highest honors, including the British George Cross, the French *Croix de Guerre* and *Légion d'Honneur*, and the American Medal of Freedom. She was, despite the accolades, clear about the incidental value of medals, saying, "I didn't fight for medals; I fought for freedom." And when pressed by the Australian government to accept further awards, she said, "They can stick them where the monkey put the nuts"—the meaning of which is clear enough.

A socialite with a mission

Nancy, the youngest of six children born of a loveless marriage, spent her first months in Wellington, New Zealand, before the family moved to Sydney, Australia. Nancy adored her father, but in an interview, she said of him: "He was very good-looking. But he was a bastard." After he had walked out on his family, Nancy was left in the care of her deeply religious, stiflingly middle-class mother. At 16 she ran away from home and trained to be a nurse. Then an unexpected legacy from an aunt allowed her to do what she'd always wanted: to leave Australia and see the world.

A self-schooled journalist, she traveled to New York and London and then across Europe, enjoying every second of her freedom. But it was not all fun and parties. During the 1930s she witnessed the rise of the Nazis in Germany and Austria, developing a deep loathing of their violently anti-Semitic ideology. In November 1939, now in France, Wake married wealthy French businessman Henri Fiocca (1898–1943), settling in the southern French port of Marseilles.

Chasing the White Mouse

After France's surrender, Nancy and Henri joined the emerging French Resistance movement. Nancy worked as a courier and became part of Ian Garrow (1908–76) and Albert Guérisse's (1911–89) escape network, known as the "Pat Line" (see Feature, opposite). Her ability to evade arrest and escape when she was in custody led the *Gestapo* to give her the nickname the White Mouse. In the aftermath of Operation Torch, the Germans occupied Vichy France and the *Gestapo* redoubled their efforts to capture Wake, offering a 5-million-franc reward for her capture. When Guérisse was arrested in 1943, she decided that it was time to escape to England. Henri stayed behind, and was arrested, tortured, and executed by the *Gestapo*. After a short period of arrest in Toulouse and several failed attempts to leave France by walking across the Pyrenees, she finally made it to Spain, and from there to London.

BELOW:
One of Wake's many exploits was cycling 310 miles (500km) across enemy territory, and bluffing her way through German and Vichy checkpoints to restore radio links with London.

FEATURE | **The Pat Line**

In the movie *Casablanca* (1942), all that Ingrid Bergman and Paul Henreid need to escape from Vichy-controlled Morocco are the letters of transit that Humphrey Bogart chivalrously hands over to his rival. But for enemies of the Reich—Jews, political dissidents, and foreign servicemen—the reality of escaping from Vichy France was far more dangerous and difficult. Lieutenant Ian Garrow, who had become stranded in France after Dunkirk, walked the 625 miles (1,000km) from

Normandy to Marseilles, and handed himself in to the Vichy authorities. Although interned, he was free to move around the city and was able to organize an escape network for British internees, POWs, and downed airmen. He was assisted by Nancy Wake and Belgian SOE agent Albert Guérisse, who took over the network after Garrow's arrest by the Vichy police in October 1941. The network became known as the Pat Line, after Guérisse's wartime alias, Patrick O'Leary.

Nazi killer

Described by SOE's Vera Atkins as "a real Australian bombshell," Wake was a natural undercover agent: a crack shot who excelled in fieldcraft and was always in high spirits. At the end of April 1944, she was parachuted into the central French region of the Auvergne, where she joined the local Resistance group led by Captain Henri Tardivat. When he found her stuck up a tree and paid her a sexist compliment, she retorted, "Don't give me that French sh*t!"

Wake's original mission was to allocate equipment and funds to the Resistance, but she was not the kind of woman who stayed in camp while the men went to fight. When the group lost their radio codes during a German raid, she cycled 310 miles (500km) across enemy territory, bluffing and flirting her way through numerous checkpoints, to restore communications with London.

She also took an active role in attacks on enemy installations. In one raid on a *Gestapo* HQ, Wake killed a German sentry with a single karate chop to prevent him from raising the alarm. In an interview, she commented matter-of-factly: "They'd taught this judo-chop stuff with the flat of the hand … But this was the only time I used it—whack—and it killed him all right." On another occasion, when the leader of a Resistance unit had been killed, she and two American soldiers held the enemy off, allowing the partisans to retreat without further losses. Between April and August 1944, Wake's 7,500 partisans held down 22,000 German troops, killing 1,400, with a loss of only 100 their own.

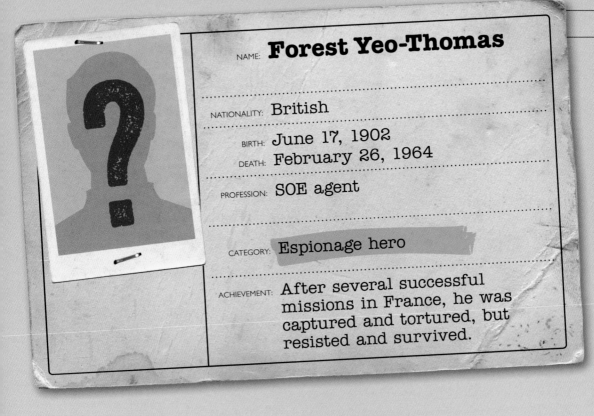

NAME: **Forest Yeo-Thomas**

NATIONALITY: British

BIRTH: June 17, 1902

DEATH: February 26, 1964

PROFESSION: SOE agent

CATEGORY: Espionage hero

ACHIEVEMENT: After several successful missions in France, he was captured and tortured, but resisted and survived.

A born adventurer, Forest Yeo-Thomas lied about his age to fight in World War I and then distinguished himself in World War II as an SOE agent in France. When captured, Churchill's "White Rabbit" resisted *Gestapo* torture and escaped to rejoin the Allied war effort.

When Ian Fleming, himself an officer with Naval Intelligence during World War II, was casting around for models for his master spy, 007, he was spoiled for choice. This section features two men whose characters and exploits are thought to have inspired Fleming's fictional MI6 agent: the urbane playboy, Soviet spymaster Richard Sorge (pp. 94–97), and the dashing soldier and ladies' man, Fitzroy Maclean

(pp. 70–73). In the current entry, we find yet more ingredients that make up Bond's distinctive character: his unquenchable thirst for adventure and danger, his joyful disregard for his own safety, and the "license to kill" that he exercised in the service of his country.

While Nancy Wake was the ever-elusive White Mouse, Yeo-Thomas was the equally hard-to-

catch White Rabbit—the character that Alice follows into and across
Wonderland. In some respects, their nicknames were well chosen, yet they
were also quite incongruous, given that the careers of both agents, and the
ease with which they killed when they needed to.

Yeo-Thomas' honors included the George Cross, only two of which were
awarded to living SOE agents (the other being Odette Sansom, pp. 88–89),
the *Croix de Guerre* and the *Légion d'Honneur*. But like other veterans of
wartime espionage, his postwar career was marred by worsening episodes of
physical and psychological ill health. The man who had lived for danger and
excitement died in peacetime at the relatively young age of 62.

BELOW:
Yeo-Thomas was
instrumental in reinforcing
General de Gaulle's position
as leader of the Free French
when he reported on the
state of the Resistance to
Winston Churchill.

No Forest Gump

London-born Forest Yeo-Thomas moved with his family to the French
port of Dieppe on the Channel coast and grew up bilingual in English
and French. Aged 16, he lied about his age to enlist with the American
Expeditionary Forces and fought on the Western Front. Still a teenager,
he went to fight with the Poles in the Polish–Soviet War (1919–20).
Captured and condemned to death by
the Russians, he escaped by strangling
a Russian guard.

Back in Paris, he married Lillian
Walker, with whom he had two
daughters. He worked in banking until
1932, when he got a job working for
Edward Molyneux, a former British
officer and couturier established in Paris.
At the outbreak of war, he enlisted in the
RAF, but ironically, considering his
underage service, he was considered too
old for a frontline role at the age of 37.

Instead he went to France as an RAF intelligence officer and interpreter.
After the fall of France and the evacuation of British forces from Dunkirk,
he worked as an interpreter for General Charles de Gaulle's Free French
forces in London.

Churchill and the White Rabbit

With his military and intelligence experience and fluent French, Yeo-Thomas was an ideal candidate for SOE's F-Section, which recruited him in February 1942. A year later, after working as a liaison officer with the Free French *Bureau Central de Renseignements et d'Action* (BCRA), he was sent to France on his first mission, accompanying de Gaulle's intelligence chief, André Dewavrin (pp. 140–143), and French journalist and Resistance leader Pierre Brossolette (pp. 132–135), on a fact-finding mission about the various Resistance groups in occupied France.

During another tour of Resistance movements with Brossolette in September 1943, when he traveled under the codename "White Rabbit," Yeo-Thomas was shocked by the lack of financial and material support that the Resistance was receiving from the Allies. Having left Brossolette in France, he requested and obtained a meeting with Prime Minister Winston Churchill, receiving the PM's assurance that he would increase British support for the Resistance.

FEATURE   ## Hitler's terror police

There comes a moment in every World War II spy movie, when the protagonists are subjected to the horror of the *Gestapo*, the Nazi's *Geheime Staatspolizei* (secret state police), which dealt with the regime's opponents inside and outside the Reich and maintained discipline within the Nazi Party. Founded in 1933 by Hitler's close associate and later head of the *Luftwaffe*, Hermann Göring, it was incorporated into Heinrich Himmler's SS a year later. From 1939 onward, both the *Gestapo* and its sister organization, the SD, became organs of a centralized *Reichs Hauptsicherheitsamt*, or RHSA (Reich Main Security Office). The *Gestapo* consisted of five departments: "A"—Political Opponents (within the Reich); "B"—Sects and Churches; "C"—Administration and Party Affairs; "D"—Occupied Territories (reproducing departments A and B in occupied Europe); and "E"—Counterintelligence (divided into Policy Formation, the West, Scandinavia, the East, and the South).

Licensed to kill

Not long after his meeting with Churchill, Yeo-Thomas learned that Brossolette had been arrested. He was determined to rescue his friend, even though his senior position in F-Section meant that, if he were captured, he would pose a major security risk to SOE agents in France and to the Resistance. Yeo-Thomas parachuted into France at the end of February 1944, but before he could rescue Brossolette, who died in custody a few hours later, he was betrayed and arrested by the *Gestapo* (see Feature, opposite). He was subjected to brutal torture, including water-boarding and electric shocks, but stuck to his story that he was a downed RAF pilot.

After interrogation, he was transferred to prison in France. Two weeks before the liberation of Paris, he and another 36 SOE and French agents were taken to Buchenwald concentration camp. In September 1944, 16 members of Yeo-Thomas's group were executed and it became clear that the survivors needed to escape to avoid the same fate. In the end, only three of the original 36 managed to escape, with the help of an SS doctor who furnished them with false identities. Posing as a French soldier, Yeo-Thomas was moved to a POW camp, from where he escaped in April 1945.

By May 8, he was back in Paris, and though he had not fully recovered from his imprisonment and escape, he persuaded SOE to send him on Operation Outhaul, a mission to track down concentration camp guards who were hiding in Germany. But when SOE realized that Outhall might be little more than Yeo-Thomas' private vendetta against the men who had tortured and imprisoned him, it canceled the operation and recalled him back to France.

ABOVE:
After his arrest and brutal interrogation by the *Gestapo*, Yeo-Thomas and another 36 SOE and French agents were transferred to Buchenwald concentration camp.

Resistance heroes

The Nazi Reich was extremely good at generating both internal and external resistance to its oppressive rule. The words "Resistance heroes" will make many readers think of the French Resistance, which fought a long and bloody campaign against the Nazis and their Vichy stooges, working closely with the British SOE. But there were resistance movements all over Europe, and the struggle was bitterest in eastern Europe, where entire communities battled to ensure their very survival. Within the borders of the Reich, the Nazis were opposed by political opponents from the left and persecuted groups, such as the Jews, the Roma, and members of the LGBT community. But opposition to Hitler also came from much more conservative circles: the German churches, the landed gentry, and the officer corps of the armed forces. Hitler, though he would ultimately be defeated and forced to commit suicide, escaped numerous assassination plots, and it was the plotters who met their deaths.

NAME: **Mordechai Anielewicz**

NATIONALITY: Polish

BIRTH: 1919 (exact date unknown)
DEATH: May 8, 1943 (presumed date)

PROFESSION: Resistance fighter

CATEGORY: Resistance hero

ACHIEVEMENT: He died leading the Jewish military resistance during the Warsaw Ghetto Uprising.

A member of an international Zionist youth movement, Mordechai Anielewicz opposed the German occupation of Poland by organizing the Jewish armed resistance. He returned to Warsaw in 1942 to lead the ZOB, the Jewish Fighters Organization, and died fighting to prevent the mass deportation and murder of the inhabitants of the city's Jewish Ghetto.

One of the best-kept German secrets of World War II was not something of major military significance, but rather the genocidal "Final Solution," now known as the Holocaust in the Anglo-Saxon world and the *Shoah* in Israel.

After Hitler came to power in 1933, the Nazis began the persecution of the Jewish population and other minority groups. But though they stole Jewish money and property and took away Jewish livelihoods, they usually stopped short of murdering Jews, preferring to encourage them to leave the territories controlled by the Reich. The fortunate few made it to the safety of the USA, the UK, and Mandatory Palestine, but many decided to stay, were unable to leave, or did not go far enough to escape the SS and its death squads.

The Final Solution agreed at the Wannsee Conference of January 20, 1942, was the last, most brutal, and most systematic phase of the Holocaust, implemented in all areas under the direct control of Germany. Among the worst hit was Poland's 3.5 million-strong Jewish community, which the Germans had concentrated in ghettos in the country's major cities.

Caught between two enemies

Mordechai Anielewicz did not have military training before World War II. He was the son of a poor Jewish family from the small town of Wyszków, near Warsaw. After finishing school, he joined Hashomer Hatzair, an international Socialist-Zionist youth movement founded before the World War I, whose program included the return of the Jews to Mandatory Palestine (now the states of Israel and Palestine).

In September 1939, when the Germans invaded Poland, Anielewicz and other members of Hashomer Hatzair fled eastward, hoping that the Polish armed forces would slow or halt the German advance. At this critical juncture for the survival of an independent Polish state, the Soviet Union invaded eastern Poland. Although Nazi Germany and Communist Russia were Europe's bitterest ideological rivals, they signed in 1939 a nonaggression pact, which included secret clauses that agreed the dismemberment of Poland in the event of war.

ABOVE:
Mordechai Anielewicz in his Hashomer Hatzair uniform, photographed in happier days in Warsaw in 1937, with several other future leaders of the Warsaw Ghetto uprising.

Underground leader

With Poland occupied by its two largest neighbors, Anielewicz tried to open an escape route to Mandatory Palestine through neighboring Romania for members of Hashomer Hatzair. But he was arrested and imprisoned by the

BELOW:
Once the Final Solution
had been decreed, the
extermination of the Jews
began all over Europe.
Jews were marched out of
Poland's ghettos and taken
to Himmler's death camps.

Soviets, who were collaborating with the Germans in suppressing all Polish resistance. Once released, he made a brief visit to Warsaw, before traveling to Wilno (now Vilnius, capital of Lithuania), where many members of Hashomer Hatzair had sought refuge. He appealed to his comrades to return to Warsaw to continue the fight against the Nazis.

Back in the ghetto, Anielewicz used his contacts and prewar position as a youth leader to organize the resistance. At first, his activities were limited to education, public meetings, lectures, and the production of underground publications in the capital and other occupied cities, but as news of the mass killings of Jews in other parts of eastern Europe and

FEATURE **Fighting to save the Warsaw Ghetto**

The other paramilitary group that fought alongside the ZOB in the Warsaw Ghetto Uprising was the *Zydowski Zwiazek Wojskowy* (ZZW; Jewish military union). The ZZW came into being in November 1939, and was formed by former members of the armed forces, as a specifically Jewish group within the Polish Resistance. In January 1940, it received the blessing of General Władysław Sikorski (1881–1943), leader of the Polish government-in-exile in London. The ZZW started with just 39 men, each armed with a semi-automatic pistol, but it grew to become one of the largest Jewish resistance groups in Poland, with units in every major city. By April 1943, when the battle for the Warsaw Ghetto's survival began, ZZW had about 500 armed fighters in the ghetto itself, bunkers to protect its members, and tunnels dug under the ghetto walls to maintain contact with the outside world and as conduits for weapons.

Russia reached Poland, he began to organize the Jewish armed resistance and established links with the Polish government-in-exile in London and the non-Jewish resistance networks outside the Warsaw Ghetto.

The uprising

In the summer of 1942, when Anielewicz was visiting resistance groups in southwest Poland, the Germans were conducting the largest deportation of Jews from the Warsaw Ghetto to the Treblinka death camp. Anielewicz returned to the city to find that the population of the ghetto had been decimated, reduced from 350,000 to around 60,000. Knowing full well that it was only a matter of time before the Germans came for the survivors, Anielewicz took over the leadership of the *Żydowska Organizacja Bojowa* (ZOB; the Jewish Fighters Organization), which fought alongside the ZZW (see Feature, opposite) in the armed struggle against the Nazis.

With weapons supplied by the non-Jewish Home Army, the ZOB prepared to resist the second major deportation of Jews planned for January 18, 1943. When the German columns were inside the ghetto, the ZOB and ZZW fighters attacked them with handguns and Molotov cocktails. Despite heavy Jewish losses, the Germans were forced to abandon the operation.

The final German assault, led in its closing stages by SS general Jurgen Stroop (1895–1952), came on April 19, 1943. Despite the overwhelming superiority of the Germans, who had the advantage in terms of numbers and firepower, the

BELOW:
Monument to the Warsaw Ghetto Uprising.

Jewish fighters were initially victorious in the battle for the ghetto's narrow streets. Stroop ordered the systematic burning of the ghetto, house by house, street by street. The fighters withdrew to their bunkers, where many died of suffocation. Four weeks after the uprising had begun, Stroop reported, "There is no more Jewish quarter in Warsaw." The ghetto was a smoking ruin. Anielewicz and his remaining fighters are presumed to have died on May 8 in the ZOB HQ bunker at 18 Mila Street, now the site of a memorial to the Jewish resistance.

NAME: **Ludwig Beck**

NATIONALITY: German

BIRTH: June 29, 1880
DEATH: July 21, 1944

PROFESSION: Soldier

CATEGORY: Resistance hero

ACHIEVEMENT: He opposed Hitler's war plans and plotted to replace him as head of state.

A career soldier from a Prussian military family, Ludwig Beck was an army officer of the old school. He initially supported Hitler, as he believed he could restore military pride after the forced disarmament imposed on Germany by the Treaty of Versailles. Eventually he became disillusioned with the Nazis, and plotted to assassinate and replace Hitler.

While many of the internal enemies of the Nazi Third Reich were drawn from the Left—Communists, socialists, trade unionists, and intellectuals, and from persecuted groups, such as the Jews—there was also significant resistance to Hitler from German conservatives, in particular from within the armed forces. The Imperial German Armed Forces of the Second Reich (1871–1918) were a relatively recent creation, the amalgamation of the armies and navies of 27 independent states and free cities, which had been united under the leadership of the Prussian army. Although much diminished after Germany's defeat in World War I, when they became the *Reichswehr* (1918–35), the defense forces of the Weimar Republic (1919–35), they retained their Prussian traditions, which were retained by Hitler's rearmed *Wehrmacht* (1935–46).

Chief of the General Staff General
Ludwig Beck came from an old
Prussian military family from
Hesse-Nassau (now the State of
Hesse). A career soldier, he served
as a staff officer in the World War I,
and climbed through the ranks
until he was appointed Chief of the
General Staff in 1934, the year
Hitler cemented his hold on power.
Although he was never a member of
the Nazi Party, he was sympathetic
to its aims, in particular its pledge
to restore national pride after the defeat in World War I and to overturn the
conditions set by the Treaty of Versailles (1919), which limited the size and
equipment of Germany's armed forces.

ABOVE:
Soldiers of the German
Reichswehr march through
Berlin in 1932. Many in the
German military welcomed
the Nazis into power the
following year.

Advocate for the Nazis

Beck first met Hitler in 1930, at the trial of three of his officers who had
been arrested for distributing Nazi propaganda, at a time when members
of the *Reichswehr* were forbidden by law to belong to any political party.
Although Beck was never a Nazi Party member, he argued that the ban
on membership should be rescinded because the aims of the movement
coincided with those of many officers and men in the *Reichswehr*, who
believed that it was time for Germany to regain its position as one of
Europe's military superpowers.

At the time Germany was on the brink of economic and social collapse.
With the onset of the Great Depression in 1929, the relative prosperity of
the 1920s had evaporated, and many feared a Soviet-style revolution, as
supporters of right and left rioted on the streets and inflation spiraled out
of control. Given the choice between Communism and National Socialism,
it was natural that a military man like Beck, who like many of his comrades
had little faith in or respect for the center-left Weimar Republic (1919–35),
should side with Hitler's simplistic message of strong government and
military rearmament. When Hitler came to power in Germany in 1933,

Beck wrote exultantly: "I have wished for many years for the political revolution, and now my wishes have come true. It is the first ray of hope since 1918."

Supping with the devil

What Hitler's conservative and military supporters realized too late was that Hitler was politically just as dangerous and radical as the Communists. They had sought to use him to restore order but now they discovered that he had used them to gain absolute power. Hitler consolidated his position, playing off one conservative faction against another, but all the time increasing the influence of the Nazi Party and the SS at the expense of the armed forces.

Beck was no liberal. He advocated the immediate rearmament of Germany, breaching the conditions imposed by the Treaty of Versailles and, once she was strong enough, a series of limited wars to establish German preeminence in central and eastern Europe. He shared Hitler's dream of a "Greater German Reich" that would unite Austria and the German-speaking provinces of Czechoslovakia, but at the same time, he argued that if Hitler moved too soon, he would trigger a military response from the French and British, which would lead to a second defeat and humiliation of Germany. Through 1938, Beck made ever more urgent appeals to Hitler to reconsider his plans to invade Czechoslovakia. He preferred to believe that the *Führer* had been misled by the more radical elements in the *Wehrmacht* rather than being the real driving force behind the invasion plans. Realizing that he could not change Hitler's mind, Beck resigned in August 1938.

Overthrowing the Führer

Beck now concluded that in order to save Germany and the *Wehrmacht*, Hitler would have to be overthrown. He began plotting with other high-ranking military opponents of the regime in the *Schwarze Kapelle* (Black

FEATURE **Defenders of the Reich**

The third arm of Hitler's intelligence apparatus, alongside the *Gestapo* and the SD, was the *Abwehr*, German military intelligence. While the *Gestapo* and SD were part of the SS and thus closely integrated within the Nazi regime, the *Abwehr* retained its operational independence as part of the *Wehrmacht*. In 1920, despite a ban on the creation of a German intelligence agency stipulated by the Treaty of Versailles, the defense ministry established a clandestine intelligence and counterintelligence organization, calling it simply "Defense," *Abwehr* in German. Within Germany, the *Abwehr* had stations in each army district, and its organization mirrored that of the conventional armed forces. Overseas, the *Abwehr* used the cover of German diplomatic and trade missions to establish networks of agents. As the Reich grew, the *Abwehr's* mission expanded into occupied countries. It remained independent until 1944, when it was merged with the SD after the Canaris affair.

Orchestra) and made overtures to the British prime minister, Winston Churchill. His aim was to depose Hitler, purge the more extreme Nazi elements from the government, and negotiate a peace with Britain and France that would allow Germany to keep its territorial gains in Austria, Poland, and Czechoslovakia. In 1943 and 1944, Beck was involved in several assassination attempts on Hitler's life, including Claus von Stauffenberg's July 20 plot. Unmasked as one of the leading conspirators, Beck was ordered to commit suicide. He shot himself twice, but only succeeded in injuring himself. He had to be finished off with a bullet in the back of the neck.

ABOVE:
After his resignation, Beck—pictured here with fellow general Werner von Freiherr in 1937—stayed in touch with many high-ranking opponents of the regime and plotted Hitler's overthrow.

NAME: **Dietrich Bonhoeffer**

NATIONALITY: German

BIRTH: February 4, 1906
DEATH: April 9, 1945

PROFESSION: Lutheran pastor

CATEGORY: Resistance hero

ACHIEVEMENT: An outspoken critic of Hitler, he paid the ultimate price for defying the Nazis.

One of the leading Lutheran theologians of the 20th century, Dietrich Bonhoeffer was an early critic of Hitler. When the Evangelical Church was taken over by the Nazis, he was instrumental in setting up the dissenting Confessing Church. Arrested by the *Gestapo*, he was executed for plotting against Hitler's life.

For those of us who were brought up on a diet of simplistic 1950s and '60s American war films in which the only good German was a dead German, it is sometimes difficult to remember that not all citizens of the Reich were enthusiastic Nazis. Although many were seduced by the demagogue's rhetoric of ultranationalism, militarism, and racial superiority, men such as Lutheran pastor Dietrich Bonhoeffer understood the true nature of Nazism long before Hitler came to power in 1933.

In the previous entry, we saw that many in the higher echelons of the German military opposed Hitler, but this and the entries on Clemens von Galen (pp. 144–147) and Martin Niemöller (pp. 152–155) focus on the role of the Christian churches in the German resistance to Nazism.

Much has been made of the Nazis' interest in occultism and ancient
Germanic paganism, and though a few individuals within Hitler's inner
clique held rather unconventional religious views, it is likely that Hitler
himself was an atheist. As a supreme political pragmatist, however, he sought
to use the influence and organization of Germany's Protestant and Catholic
churches to further his own political ends.

From studying to living faith

Bonhoeffer was a gifted Christian theologian in the Lutheran Protestant
tradition. He completed his studies in theology at Berlin University, graduating
summa cum laude in 1927. He completed a further doctorate in 1929, aged 24,
a full year before he was legally of age to become an ordained minister. With a
year to fill, he decided to do a
postgraduate course at a seminary
in New York. His experiences in
the United States would shape the
course of his life and ministry.

While in New York, he met Adam
Clayton Powell, Sr. (1865–1953),
the pastor of the Abyssinian Baptist
Church in Harlem, the largest
Protestant congregation in the USA,
where Bonhoeffer taught Sunday
school. It was while in the USA,
where he witnessed the African-
American struggle for civil rights, that he began to develop his Christ-
centered theology of social justice. Having completed his course of study,
he traveled widely, across the United States and Mexico, and visited Cuba,
Libya, Italy, and Spain, developing a strong interest in ecumenism. He
returned to Germany, no longer a Christian academic but a man
determined to live his faith in his everyday life and ministry.

ABOVE:
Bonhoeffer, pictured here
with German students in
1932, traveled widely after
completing his doctorate
in theology. His experiences
led him away from an
academic approach to
religion toward a faith
founded upon lived
experience and action.

"Render unto Caesar"

In the Gospel of Matthew, Jesus defined the church's relationship to the
state with the words, "Render unto Caesar the things that are Caesar's."

FEATURE **Confessing against Hitler**

In order to achieve absolute control in Germany, the Nazis planned the takeover of all social, political, and religious institutions, including the established Evangelical churches. The *Deutsche Christen* movement—the faith wing of the Nazi Party—emerged in 1931, with the aim of ensuring the election of Nazi party members and sympathizers to key church offices. Their dominance after 1933 ensured that the Protestant churches accepted the Aryan paragraph—a key piece of legislation that banned Jews and Christians of Jewish descent from taking part in German civil society. The interference in the internal affairs of the church and the persecution of German Jews led to a schism within the Protestant movement, and the emergence of the breakaway Confessing Church that became the focus of Christian opposition to Hitler. Both Bonhoeffer and Martin Niemöller took leading roles in the Confessing Church, whose founding declaration affirmed that it would never allow itself to become an organ of the Nazi state.

In 1st-century Judea, Caesar was usually wise enough to keep out of the religious affairs of his rebellious Jewish subjects, but in 20th-century Germany, Hitler wished to control every aspect of life, including religion. To this end, the pro-Nazi *Deutsche Christen* movement engineered a takeover of the Protestant churches, triggering the creation of the dissident Confessing Church (see Feature, above). Bonhoeffer, who had been ordained in 1931, took a leading role in the new church and was the first Christian voice to denounce the Nazi persecution of German Jews.

In 1933, although rebuked by his friends for running away from the fight in Germany, Bonhoeffer, disheartened by the ease of the Nazi takeover of the church, took a two-year appointment as the pastor of two German churches in London. When he returned to Germany, the Nazis were firmly in control and determined to crush all opposition. The persecution of the Confessing Church, so vocal in its criticism of Hitler, had begun. During the next few years, many of its leaders and pastors were arrested and its seminaries closed. Bonhoeffer was left at liberty but was forbidden to teach, speak in public, write, or publish. Banned from entering Berlin, he established and taught at a network of underground seminaries in rural districts of eastern Germany.

The pastor-spy

With the outbreak of war, Bonhoeffer was recruited to join the *Abwehr*, which had been subverted by its head, Wilhelm Canaris (pp. 136–139), and was now the focus of the military resistance to Hitler. The unlikely cover of a military intelligence officer saved Bonhoeffer from conscription into the regular armed forces and allowed him to travel widely, establishing contacts with church leaders in occupied and neutral countries, acting as a courier for the Resistance, and helping German Jews to escape to neutral Switzerland.

In April 1943, Bonhoeffer's luck ran out, and he, too, was arrested, and sent to a military prison in Berlin. After Hitler found evidence of the *Abwehr* and Bonhoeffer's participation in the plots on his life, he decided that all the conspirators should be court-martialed and executed. Bonhoeffer was transferred to Flossenbürg concentration camp, where he was tried by an SS court and condemned to death by hanging on April 9, 1945, just weeks before the German surrender. Fortunately for the world and postwar Germany, Bonhoeffer continued to write throughout his imprisonment, and his many papers, letters, and poems were preserved and published.

ABOVE:
Flossenbürg concentration camp, where Bonhoeffer and leading members of the *Schwarze Kapelle*, the conservative opposition to Hitler, were executed.

NAME: **Andrée Borrel**

NATIONALITY: French

BIRTH: November 18, 1919

DEATH: July 6, 1944

PROFESSION: Member of the French Resistance and SOE agent

CATEGORY: Resistance hero

ACHIEVEMENT: An early member of the French Resistance, she later became a key SOE agent.

Andrée Borrel was typical of many ordinary French men and women who refused to accept the humiliating armistice imposed on France by a victorious Hitler in June 1940. Forced to flee the country, she joined de Gaulle's Free French and then SOE. Captured and tortured, she died a true hero of the French Resistance.

Before 1940, France and the main German power, the Kingdom of Prussia, had been fighting wars for centuries, sometimes as enemies and sometimes as allies. But after the French Revolution of 1789, and more particularly, after Emperor Napoleon I's (1769–1821) crushing defeat of Prussia in 1806, it became a real grudge match between the two nations, replayed several times with different outcomes. In 1871, after defeating Napoleon III's (1808–73) Second Empire, Prussia compounded the injury by choosing to stage the unification of the Second German Reich in the Hall of Mirrors of the Palace of Versailles. In 1919, the French handsomely repaid the insult by imposing on Germany the humiliating terms of the Treaty of Versailles, pointedly using the same venue to wipe out their earlier humiliation.

Hitler's six-week defeat of the French army in the summer of 1940 shocked Europe and so demoralized the French that the majority of the population acquiesced in the defeat, and many French citizens chose to collaborate with the Germans and the puppet government installed in Vichy under the leadership of Marshal Philippe Pétain (1856–1951). The country was divided into the German-occupied north and west, and the nominally independent Vichy south. As in Germany, the Resistance first emerged among groups that expected little mercy from the Nazis: Communists, Socialists, Jews, and those in the armed forces who refused to accept the armistice, headed by General Charles de Gaulle, who established the Free French government-in-exile in London in the summer of 1940.

ABOVE:
Adolf Hitler posing in front of the iconic Eiffel Tower in Paris. Many French men and women, like Borrel, refused to accept France's defeat in 1940.

The girl from Louveciennes

Andrée Borrel was not from a grand political dynasty or an old military family. She was an ordinary working-class girl from the suburbs of Paris who worked in a department store and loved to cycle competitively in her spare time. Just before the war, she moved with her ailing mother to the port of Toulon in the south of France. At the outbreak of war, she joined the Red Cross and worked as a nurse caring for wounded French servicemen.

When France surrendered in June 1940, Borrel and her partner, Lieutenant Maurice Dufour, refused to accept their country's defeat and joined the fledgling French Resistance. They rented a villa near Perpignan, close to the Spanish border, which was used as one of the Pat Line's safe houses (see Feature, p. 109). When a captured British agent betrayed the network, Borrel escaped to Spain and then Portugal, where she spent several months working for the Free French propaganda office in Lisbon. In April 1942, she reached London, where she hoped to join de Gaulle.

ABOVE:
As soon as the armistice
between Germany and Vichy
France had been signed,
thousands of French citizens
joined the Resistance or
went to London to join
the Free French.

Denise meets Prosper

Although rejected by the Free French, who were suspicious of her leftwing views, she was recruited by SOE's F-Section. Once trained, Borrel, codenamed "Denise," and fellow agent Lise de Baissac (1905–2004), codenamed "Odile," were the first two female SOE operatives to be parachuted into France. Because she had worked in Paris before the war and knew the city well, Borrel was sent to prepare for the arrival of the head of the "Prosper" network (see Feature, below), SOE agent Francis Suttill (1910–45).

During the nine months of Prosper's existence, Borrel supervised weapons drops and took part in sabotage operations. Impressed by his young French recruit, Suttill made her the second in command of Prosper's Paris group, and was fulsome in his praise of her when he spoke to his superiors in London.

Unfortunately, the network had been betrayed to the Germans, possibly by French double agent Henri Déricourt (1909–62). Although Déricourt was tried for collaboration and treason after the war, his betrayal could not be proved and he was acquitted. Between June and October 1943, most of the

---

FEATURE ## A less than prosperous outcome

The "Prosper" network was typical of a joint SOE–Resistance operation. Established in the fall of 1942, it would operate for nine months until June 1943, when it was betrayed to the Germans and many of its agents were arrested and executed. The head of the network was British SOE agent, Francis Suttill, also codenamed "Prosper," who parachuted into France on October 2, 1942. Headquartered in Paris, the network ran Resistance groups all over northern and central France and in western Belgium. At its height it had some 1,300 operatives, including SOE agents acting as couriers and radio operators. Prosper mounted several successful sabotage operations, including the bombing of enemy installations, the destruction of electricity pylons, and the derailment of trains carrying German troops and war supplies. It also organized equipment and weapons drops, and operated clandestine airfields for the transport of SOE personnel to and from England.

LEFT:
After her arrest and
torture, Borrel was
murdered in the Struthof-
Natzweiler concentration
camp, the only German
concentration camp built
on French soil.

members of the network were arrested. Among the last was to be captured was Noor-un-Nisa Inayat Khan (pp. 66–69), who had remained at her post in Paris despite the offer of repatriation to England.

The fall of Prosper

Borrel was among the first to be arrested by the *Gestapo* in Paris on the night of June 23–24, along with the network's radio operator Gilbert Norman (1914–44). The following morning, Suttill was arrested in his Paris hotel. Borrel was taken to SD HQ in central Paris for interrogation, and then transferred to Fresnes prison, which already held several SOE agents.

On May 12, 1944, Borrel and seven other female SOE agents, including Odette Sansom (pp. 88–89), who would be the group's only survivor, were chained together in pairs and deported to Germany by train. Borrel and three other female agents were taken to Struthof-Natzweiler concentration camp in occupied Alsace. Soon after their arrival on July 6, the women were given a lethal injection of phenol, and their bodies burned in the crematorium ovens. But according to eyewitness testimony, Borrel did not die from the injection and fought her executioner, injuring him before he succeeded in forcing her into the oven where she was burned alive. She was 24 years of age. Her posthumous awards included the French *Croix de Guerre* and the British King's Commendation for Brave Conduct.

NAME: **Pierre Brossolette**

NATIONALITY: French

BIRTH: June 25, 1903

DEATH: March 22, 1944

PROFESSION: Member of the French Resistance

CATEGORY: Resistance hero

ACHIEVEMENT: A Socialist politician, he was one of the principal organizers of the French Resistance.

A journalist and Socialist politician in prewar France, Pierre Brossolette was an early adherent to the Resistance in Paris in the first months of the occupation. In 1942, he traveled to London to meet with de Gaulle, who tasked him with uniting the Resistance groups in the northern German-occupied zone.

The history of France's postwar Fourth Republic (1946–58) was embittered by the fallout from the country's wartime defeat, which saw large segments of the French population passively acquiesce in or actively collaborate with the German occupation and the collaborationist Vichy regime between 1940 and 1944. After an initial period of violent reprisals and the prosecutions of the worst collaborators, the French settled into a decade of soul-searching and self-doubt, from which even the dead were not immune. In a country riven by the great ideological divide between the conservative Christian democrats and Gaullists on one side and the Socialists and Communists on the other, the minutiae of who had fought in which Resistance movement, and exactly when they had joined the fight, became political ammunition in parliamentary and media firefights.

For decades, Jean Moulin (pp. 148–151) was hailed as the great hero and organizer of the French Resistance, and Socialist activist and journalist Pierre Brossolette's equally important contribution in creating the *Conseil National de la Résistance* (CNR) was downplayed. However, the two men had performed very similar roles, Moulin in southern Vichy France and Brossolette in occupied northern France. In 2015, his services to France received the ultimate accolade, when his remains were transferred to France's national mausoleum, the Panthéon, where they now rest alongside Jean Moulin's ashes.

From peace to war

Like many intellectuals belonging to the prewar French left, Brossolette was a great believer in the sacred primacy of human rights, the fight against anti-Semitism, and the pacifist ideals of Nobel Prize winner for Peace and secretary of the League of Nations Aristide Briand (1862–1932), who tried to make war illegal. An active member of the SFIO, later the French Socialist Party, Brossolette worked as an adviser to Socialist ministers in government and as a journalist and editor with leftwing newspapers and for the French state broadcaster, Radio PTT.

ABOVE:
Collaboration with the German occupiers led to a terrible fallout in postwar France. Here, French militiamen loyal to the Vichy regime hold partisans captive.

In 1938, he woke up to the grave threat posed by the fascist regimes in Germany and Italy. A year later, he was fired from Radio PTT for denouncing the Munich Agreement between Germany, Italy, France, and Britain, which allowed Hitler to take over the German-speaking provinces of Czechoslovakia. At the outbreak of war, he was drafted into the armed forces, serving as a lieutenant in the infantry until the fall of France. In July 1941, he was the recipient of the first French *Croix de Guerre*, awarded because he managed to retreat with his unit, without any loss of personnel or equipment.

FEATURE **The first embers**

The *Musée de l'Homme* network, one of the first Resistance groups to emerge in France after the defeat of June 1940, was not established by ex-soldiers or Communist partisans, but by a group of scientists, librarians, and academics attached to several major institutions in Paris, including the *Bibliothèque Nationale*, France's national library, and the *Musée de l'Homme*, the national museum of anthropology. The joint organizers of the network were anthropologist Anatole Lewitsky (1903–42) and ethnographer Boris Vildé (1908–42). So as not to attract undue attention from the *Gestapo* and SD, the group operated under the cover of a literary society— the "Friends of Alain Fournier"—named for the famous French novelist who died fighting the Germans in 1914. The group published an underground newspaper, *Résistance*, and fostered contacts with other networks in occupied France. When the group was infiltrated by an SD agent in 1941, most of its members were arrested and imprisoned or executed.

Founding the French Resistance

An opponent of the Vichy regime from its creation, Brossolette joined the *Musée de l'Homme Resistance* network (see Feature, left). He wrote the last issue of the group's newsletter, *Résistance*, in March 1941, narrowly avoiding capture when the SD infiltrated the network and arrested its leaders. He took part in the organization of several armed resistance groups in German-occupied France, and under the codename "Pedro" became head of press and propaganda for Gilbert Renault's (pp. 158–161) Confrérie Notre-Dame Resistance network. With his wife he purchased a bookshop in Paris, which was used as a central "post office" for the various Resistance groups in the Paris region.

In April 1942, he traveled to London to meet de Gaulle, who made him a major in the BCRA (see Feature, p. 142). He began to work closely with SOE, establishing a close friendship with Forest Yeo-Thomas (pp. 110–113). In 1942–43, Brossolette went to France three times. Together with Yeo-Thomas and André Dewavrin (pp. 140–143), Brossolette began the work of uniting the disparate Resistance groups in the occupied zone and linking them to those brought together by Jean Moulin in Vichy France into the overarching *Conseil National de la Résistance*.

A friend in need

In February 1944, Brossolette attempted to return to England to report to de Gaulle about the progress he was making with the CNR. After several failed attempts to rendezvous with planes that would have flown him to London, he

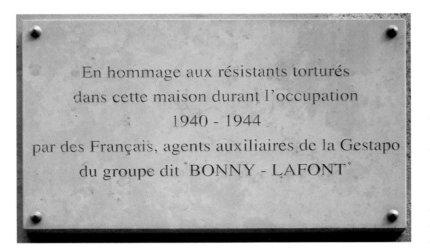

En hommage aux résistants torturés
dans cette maison durant l'occupation
1940 - 1944
par des Français, agents auxiliaires de la Gestapo
du groupe dit 'BONNY - LAFONT'

LEFT:

A plaque at the site of the French *Gestapo* in Paris, commemorating "the members of the Resistance tortured in this house during the occupation 1940–1944."

boarded a boat in Brittany with a group of escaping British servicemen but fell into enemy hands after the boat was wrecked in bad weather. He was not recognized as one of the SD's most wanted Resistance leaders for several weeks, which gave his close friend Yeo-Thomas the opportunity to plan an audacious rescue attempt. Unfortunately a poorly coded French radio transmission broke Brossolette's cover, and he was transferred from Brittany to *Gestapo* HQ in Paris for interrogation.

ABOVE:

A fake identity card used by Pierre Brossolette during one of his missions to France to unite the disparate Resistance groups in the National Resistance Council.

As Yeo-Thomas' rescue mission turned to disaster, and the would-be rescuer was himself arrested, tortured, and imprisoned, Brossolette was exposed to the full brutality of the *Gestapo*. During a break in his interrogation, Brossolette was left alone in a small room on the top floor of the *Gestapo* HQ in Paris. Bound to a chair and terrified that he would break under torture and betray his friends, he lifted the chair and threw himself out of the window. He fell onto a fourth-floor balcony, seriously injuring himself. He died that evening in hospital without recovering consciousness.

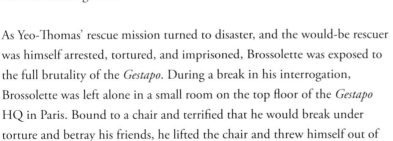

NAME: **Wilhelm Canaris**

NATIONALITY: German

BIRTH: January 1, 1887
DEATH: April 9, 1945

PROFESSION: Head of the *Abwehr*

CATEGORY: Resistance hero

ACHIEVEMENT: He subverted German military intelligence, using it to oppose Hitler and plot his assassination.

A career officer in the German Navy who had served with distinction in World War I, Wilhelm Canaris initially supported Hitler because he saw him as the only person capable of restoring order in Germany. Disillusioned, he used his position as head of the *Abwehr* to thwart Hitler at every turn.

The phrase, "If you can't beat them, join them," is typically understood to be defeatist in nature. Admiral Wilhelm Canaris, head of the *Abwehr* (German military intelligence) from 1935 to 1944, turned this on its head and decided that if he wanted to beat Hitler, the best way to do it was to appear to join him. In his background, experience, and views, he had a lot in common with fellow conspirator in the *Schwarze Kapelle*, General Ludwig Beck (pp. 120–123). In contrast to Beck, however, he opted for a completely different *modus operandi*.

Beck was an old-school army officer who, when he finally realized he could not change Hitler's mind, and had, in fact, misjudged him all along, did the honorable thing and resigned as Chief of the General Staff before Hitler took Germany to war with Poland and Czechoslovakia. Beck would have been unable to stay in his post and play along with an increasingly paranoid and insane Hitler, while all the time undermining his authority and countermanding his orders. This, however, was effectively the game that Canaris played for almost the whole duration of the European war.

Saving Germany from Communism

Like the Hessian Beck, Canaris came from an old Prussian military family from Westphalia (now part of the state of North Rhine-Westphalia). It was his mistaken belief that he was related to a renowned freedom-fighting Greek admiral, with whom he shared a name, that persuaded the young Canaris to enlist in the Imperial German Navy in 1905. During World War I, he served as an intelligence officer aboard a German cruiser and saw action in the south Atlantic against the Royal Navy. In 1915, the cruiser was sunk and her crew taken prisoner and transported to Latin America. Canaris showed considerable bravery, and no little skill, in escaping from internment in Chile and returning to Germany. A gifted linguist, he was sent as a spy to Spain, and later became a noted U-boat captain with 18 kills to his name.

BELOW:
After serving with distinction in Germany's WWI U-boat fleet, Canaris was appointed Captain of the Deutschland-class battleship *SMS Schlesien*.

Like many other professional military men, Canaris felt betrayed by Germany's surrender and what he saw as the humiliating conditions imposed by the Treaty of Versailles. He was one of the organizers of the *Freikorps* (paramilitary units) made up of ex-servicemen, who successfully opposed the Communist German Revolution (1918–19), which sought to establish a Soviet-style regime. Although no democrat, he joined the Weimar Republic's *Reichsmarine* (German navy), earning swift promotion through the ranks to become captain of the battleship *Schlesien*. He was sympathetic to the aims of the Nazis during their rise to power in the early 1930s, but, again like Beck, he chose not to join the Party.

Fooling Hitler

Canaris was a Nazi fellow traveler until 1937. Hitler trusted him implicitly, promoting him to the rank of admiral and appointing him head of the *Abwehr* in 1935. By 1938, Canaris had turned against Hitler, convinced that his planned invasion of Czechoslovakia would lead to a swift German defeat. Many in the anti-Nazi camp hoped to use the Munich Crisis to mount a military coup to depose Hitler and expel the Nazis from office. Canaris was bitterly disappointed when Britain and France chose appeasement by signing the Munich Agreement, which allowed Germany to annex the German-speaking Czechoslovak Sudetenland. Emboldened, Hitler continued his plans to invade the rest of Czechoslovakia and Poland.

At the beginning of 1939, however, Canaris succeeded in stiffening British resolve. He led the British government to believe that Hitler was planning an invasion of the Netherlands in order to use it as the base for a bombing campaign so devastating that it would prevent Britain from supporting France against Germany in the forthcoming war.

After the outbreak of hostilities, Canaris, shocked by news of the war crimes being committed in Poland, became even more determined to bring an end to Hitler's rule by any means at his disposal. While appearing to be completely loyal, he plotted with other *Wehrmacht* officers to overthrow and later assassinate Hitler. At the same time, he subverted an *Abwehr* operation in the USA, negotiated with the British about possible surrender terms if he could eliminate Hitler, foiled a plot to kidnap and murder Pope Pius XII

(1876–1958; see Feature, below), and saved Jews and opponents of the regime by giving them *Abwehr* credentials, which allowed them to travel to neutral countries.

BELOW:
Canaris was able to play
a double game until 1944,
when he was implicated
in the last major Black
Orchestra attempt on
Hitler's life, the July 20 plot.

Fall from grace

Although Canaris was never directly implicated in any of the 10–15 assassination plots against Hitler, and he was under house arrest during Stauffenberg's ill-fated July 20 plot, many of the plotters were his close friends, which was enough to condemn him by association. Heinrich Himmler, who had long suspected that Canaris was a traitor, persuaded Hitler to dismiss him as head of the *Abwehr* and to merge military intelligence with his own SD.

This brilliant man, who had managed to deceive Hitler and his counterintelligence chiefs, died when almost on the brink of salvation. Himmler kept Canaris alive to negotiate with the British, but when his overtures failed, the SS leader had him court-martialed. He was condemned to death by hanging. The sentence was carried on April 9, 1945, at Flossenbürg concentration camp. Among the other men executed with him was Pastor Dietrich Bonhoeffer (pp. 124–127).

FEATURE | **A plot against the Pope**

Even by the standards of Germany's increasingly desperate efforts during the last two years of the European war, their plot to kidnap and murder Pope Pius XII to punish the Italian people for having deposed *Il Duce*, Benito Mussolini, seems bizarre in the extreme. Yet, in their depositions to the Nuremberg Trials (1945–46), two senior German officers reported different versions of the same plot. In the first, SS General Karl Wolff (1900–84) claimed to have been ordered by Hitler to kidnap the pontiff to prevent him falling into Allied hands, but to have disobeyed and warned him instead. In the second, Colonel Erwin von Lahousen (1897–1955) claimed that a plot to murder Pius had been foiled by Admiral Wilhelm Canaris, who had exposed the plot to his Italian opposite number during a secret meeting in Venice in July 1943.

NAME: **André Dewavrin**

NATIONALITY: French

BIRTH: June 9, 1911
DEATH: December 20, 1998

PROFESSION: Head of the BCRA

CATEGORY: Resistance hero

ACHIEVEMENT: He led the Free French intelligence bureau and helped organize the French Resistance.

A career soldier, André Dewavrin fought the Germans in France and Norway before making his way to London to join General de Gaulle's Free French government-in-exile. He became the first head of the Free French intelligence bureau, the BCRA, and traveled to France to help organize the Resistance.

The Germans marched unopposed into Paris on June 14, 1940. On June 17, the future leader of the Free French, General Charles de Gaulle, arrived in London, and on June 18, he made an impassioned address to the French people via the BBC, exhorting them to resist the occupier and to refuse to support the collaborationist Vichy regime headed by Marshal Pétain. According to postwar Gaullist legend, the speech marked the beginnings of the fight back against the Germans and the beginnings of the French Resistance. The reality in the first three years of the war was slightly more complex.

General de Gaulle was not the only Frenchman with ambitions to lead and unite the Resistance, and thus become France's postwar leader-in-waiting. He had a difficult relationship with his

two principal allies, Britain and the
United States. Although he had the
grudging support and respect of Prime
Minister Winston Churchill, Supreme
Allied Commander Dwight D.
Eisenhower (1890–1969) favored
another anti-Vichy general, Henri
Giraud (1879–1949), installing him
as leader of Free French forces in
North Africa after Operation Torch
(November 1942).

It was vital for de Gaulle that he be seen as
the leader of the French Resistance. This
he achieved with the help of Jean Moulin
(pp. 148–151) and Pierre Brossolette
(pp. 132–135), the co-founders of the *Conseil
National de la Résistance* (CNR). But until his
position was completely secure, he not only
needed to know what the Germans were doing,
he also needed to keep a close eye on 'rival'
Resistance networks of both the left and right, the
leaders of which might challenge his leadership.
He entrusted this delicate task to his intelligence
chief, André Dewavrin.

ABOVE:
General de Gaulle was not
the only possible leader of
the Free French and French
president-in-waiting. He had
a rival in General Henri
Giraud (far left) who had
American backing.

BELOW:
Marshal Pétain, a hero of
France's Verdun campaign
during WWI, signed the
armistice with Hitler and
became head of the
German-sponsored
Vichy regime.

Tinker, tailor, soldier, spy

Unlike the other members of the French
Resistance featured in this section, Dewavrin was
a career officer in the French army. A graduate of
the prestigious *École Polytechnique*, he opted for a
career as an officer in the *Génie*, the French army
corps of engineers. Promoted to Captain in 1938,
he was appointed as professor at the elite officer
training school of Saint-Cyr, specializing in
defensive fortifications.

FEATURE **The general's spies**

What every self-respecting national government needs—even if it doesn't actually have its own territory to govern—is an intelligence service. With whatever civilian and military intelligence capability within France in the hands of the collaborationist Vichy regime, General de Gaulle's Free French government in London established the *Bureau Central de Renseignements et d'Action* (BCRA) in July 1940. The general appointed Major André Dewavrin to head of the Bureau. The BCRA consisted of five sections: *Renseignement* (R), information gathering; *Action Militaire* (A/M) military action, which worked closely with SOE on military operations in occupied and Vichy France; *Contre-espionnage* (C/E), counterintelligence; *Évasion* (E), escape; and *Politique* or *Non Militaire* (N/M), political division for all nonmilitary matters. In 1943 the BCRA was merged with the French military intelligence organization in liberated French North Africa and became the *Direction Générale des Services Spéciaux*, the forerunner of the French postwar intelligence service.

When France declared war on Germany in September 1939, Dewavrin commanded a company of army engineers in Meaux, northeastern France, and was then transferred to the French Ninth Army at Verviers in Belgium. He also took part in the failed Allied campaign to prevent the German takeover of Norway (April–June 1940). Returning to the port of Brest in Brittany on June 17, he left immediately for England with the whole of his division.

Although Dewavrin had no background in military intelligence, he was a long-serving army officer with a strong technical background and combat experience. In any case, after the rout of the French army, de Gaulle would have had few better qualified candidates to organize and lead the Free French intelligence service, the BCRA (see Feature, left). The bureau began as an information-gathering organization, to which new functions were added, until it took its final form in the summer of 1942. The BCRA was the forerunner of the postwar French intelligence service, the *Direction Générale des Études et Recherches*, which Dewavrin would lead until 1946, when de Gaulle relinquished power to the new Fourth Republic.

Saving de Gaulle

From the point of view of his boss, Charles de Gaulle, Dewavrin's most important mission took place between February and April 1943, when, using the codename "Colonel Passy," he accompanied Forest Yeo-Thomas (pp. 110–113), who was at this time using the codename "Shelley," on a seven-week fact-finding mission

LEFT:

The ultimate betrayal of France: Pétain shaking hands with Hitler after the fall of France. The marshal was convicted of treason after the war.

on the state of the various French Resistance movements in the occupied northern zone. Once in France, they joined Pierre Brossolette (pp. 132–135), who had begun uniting the various Resistance networks in northern France. Dewavrin's key task, however, was to gauge the level of support for de Gaulle among the French Resistance and underground political parties, and to what extent they accepted his claim to be the head of the French government-in-exile.

His mission accomplished, Dewavrin returned to London on the night of April 15–16, presenting a long and detailed report to de Gaulle the next morning. The mission had been a complete success: The three men had established a coordination committee of all the groups in the northern region and laid the foundations for the Conseil National de la Resistance. On the British side, Yeo-Thomas reported to Winston Churchill that the majority of Resistance fighters accepted de Gaulle's leadership. This allowed the British premier to support the general and oppose calls from the Americans that he should be replaced. Dewavrin's final service to de Gaulle in making him indispensable to the Allied war effort was the close collaboration between the BCRA and the SOE in the planning of Operation Overlord, the Normandy landings.

NAME: **Clemens von Galen**

NATIONALITY: German

BIRTH: March 16, 1878
DEATH: March 22, 1946

PROFESSION: Catholic bishop and cardinal

CATEGORY: Resistance hero

ACHIEVEMENT: An outspoken critic of Hitler, he denounced Nazi euthanasia and the *Gestapo*.

An aristocrat and natural conservative, Catholic Bishop Clemens von Galen initially supported Hitler as a bulwark against Communism, but as he began to understand the true nature of the Nazi regime, he risked his life and liberty to denounce its euthanasia program, the *Gestapo*, and the persecution of the Catholic Church.

Historically, Germany has considerable religious baggage. It was the birthplace of the 16th-century Protestant Reformation, which triggered over a century of bloody religious wars between the German states of the Holy Roman Empire. The Peace of Westphalia that brought them to an end in 1648 created a religious patchwork, dividing Germany into Protestant and Catholic states according to the creeds of their rulers. This religious apartheid, with a more Catholic south and west and a more Protestant north and east, exacerbated political differences and held up German unification until it was railroaded through by the Lutheran Kingdom of Prussia in 1871.

During the Second Reich (1871–1918), the Evangelical Church was the country's established church, and had close ties to the ruling dynasty. But with the abdication of the Kaiser and the creation of the social-democratic Weimar Republic, the German churches lost their political roles and influence. The Feature box on page 126 describes the way the *Deutsche Christen* movement was used by the Nazis to assume control of Protestant churches. With the Catholic Church, however, the Nazis had a far more difficult task, as the organization was global and headquartered outside Germany. Despite repeated attacks and persecutions, the Catholic Church proved itself institutionally to be much more resistant to Nazism than the Evangelical Church, largely thanks to churchmen such as Clemens von Galen.

The patriotic priest

Although it is true that the Catholic clergy owe their primary allegiance to a supranational organization and leader, the Pope, this has not prevented individual churches from being fiercely nationalistic. The von Galen family, which had served the Catholic Church for centuries, were prominent members of the Catholic Westphalian nobility. One of Clemens' ancestors, and his 17th-century predecessor as Bishop of Münster, suppressed the local Anabaptists, hanging their mutilated corpses from the city walls. Young Clemens received a soundly Catholic education from the Jesuits and attended the Catholic University of Freiburg where he discovered his priestly vocation. A seminarian in the bishopric of Münster, he was ordained in 1904, and two years later was appointed to be parish priest of St. Matthias in Berlin.

ABOVE:
The von Galen family had a long association with the bishopric of Münster. One of Clemens' ancestors, as bishop of Münster, had hung the corpses of Protestants from the city walls.

During his 23-year tenure in the German capital, he witnessed World War I, which he supported enthusiastically; the fall of the German monarchy and birth of the Weimar Republic, which he feared would cause "considerable damage to Catholic Christianity"; and the rise of Soviet Stalinism, which led to the elimination of the Catholic Church in the Soviet Union. Once appointed Bishop of Münster in 1933, he supported Hitler and the Nazis, whom he viewed as steadfast opponents of Communism who would protect Germany and the Church, and also wipe out the humiliation of Germany's defeat in World War I. Although an SS guard of honor was present at his consecration and Münster Cathedral was decorated with Nazi swastikas, von Galen was never a member of the Nazi Party.

"The Lion of Münster"

Although he approved of many of Hitler's aims and policies, the new Bishop of Münster was also quick to denounce the Nazis for breaches of the 1933 *Reichskonkordat* (see Feature, opposite). He went on the offensive a year after his consecration, opposing the attempted Nazi takeover of Catholic schools and criticizing the Nazi obsession with racial purity. Most offensive from a doctrinal point of view was their attempt to suppress the Old Testament as a pre-Christian addition to the Bible rather than its foundational text, and the Nazi use of rituals inspired by Germanic paganism.

BELOW:
The papacy dealt with Hitler much as it had done with other military leaders, such as Napoleon and Mussolini, by signing a concordat that outlined the respective roles of Church and State.

Bishop von Galen, nicknamed "The Lion of Münster," resisted all pressure to curb his criticisms. In 1937, he was one of the German draftees of Pius XI's (1857–1939) encyclical, *Mit brennender Sorge* (see Feature, opposite). Nevertheless, he still regarded the Communists to be the greater threat to Germany and the Catholic Church, and when Hitler invaded Russia in 1941, he gave the *Wehrmacht*, if not its leader, his blessing.

Preaching against Hitler

In three sermons delivered from the pulpit of Münster Cathedral in July and August 1941 and then printed and distributed nationwide, von Galen made the most powerful domestic denunciations of the Nazi regime during the war. The first sermon, whose theme was "Justice is the foundation of states," exposed the extra-legal activities of the *Gestapo*; the second denounced the Nazi persecution of Catholic clergy and the confiscation of church property in breach of the articles of the *Reichskonkordat*.

He saved his strongest criticism for his third sermon, delivered on August 3, 1941. Reminding his audience of the biblical Fifth Commandment, "Thou shall not kill," he denounced the Nazis' Aktion T4 euthanasia program that eliminated over 70,000 mentally and physically disabled German citizens between 1939 and 1941. Unlike the "Final Solution," the elimination of European Jewry, which was carried on in secret in death camps outside Germany, Aktion T4 targeted patients in hospitals and asylums run by charitable bodies and churches in Germany, and so could not be kept secret from medical staff, care workers, and family members. Bishop von Galen's sermon helped expose the program within Germany.

A furious Hitler wanted von Galen eliminated, but propaganda minister Joseph Goebbels (1897–1945) argued that this would alienate too many of Germany's Catholics. The Lion of Münster was put under house arrest for the rest of the war and remained under sentence of death if Germany won. In the event, the Nazis lost and von Galen survived to be made a cardinal by Pius XII in 1946.

ABOVE:

Although Pope Pius XI was criticized for signing the *Reichskonkordat* with Hitler, he issued the anti-Nazi encyclical, *Mit brennender Sorge*, in 1937.

FEATURE | **Condemning Nazi idolatry**

The Catholic Church has been dealing with power-mad kings and emperors for over 2,000 years. In 1933 it signed the *Reichskonkordat* (1933), a treaty outlining the respective roles of Church and state in the Reich. The Nazis guaranteed the Church's independence and the safety of its clergy and property, and the church promised to stay out of politics. The Nazis, however, immediately broke the concordat, trying to impose their racist, anti-Semitic ideology in Church schools, persecuting Catholic clergy who refused to comply,

and confiscating Church property. The Church's response was the ecclesiastical equivalent of lobbing a bomb at Hitler: a papal encyclical entitled *Mit brennender Sorge* (With Burning Anxiety; 1937) that criticized Nazi neo-paganism, the idolatry of the state, and the racist ideology that decreed that Christians of Jewish descent were Jewish and subject to the Reich's draconian anti-Semitic exclusionary laws.

NAME: **Jean Moulin**

NATIONALITY: French

BIRTH: June 20, 1899

DEATH: July 8, 1943

PROFESSION: Member of the French Resistance

CATEGORY: Resistance hero

ACHIEVEMENT: He united the different factions of the French Resistance under one centralized command.

A member of the prewar French administration, Jean Moulin refused to collaborate with the Vichy regime. The Free French leader General de Gaulle entrusted him with combining the disparate movements of the French Resistance into a single national fighting force. This would become the nucleus of the postwar Fourth Republic.

Both General Ludwig Beck (pp. 120–123) and Admiral Wilhelm Canaris (pp. 136–139), two long-serving officers in the German armed forces who had fought in World War I, were convinced that if Hitler provoked a military response from France and Great Britain, Germany was bound to lose. France was among the world's wealthiest and most populous nations, with a large colonial empire, which could mobilize Europe's largest peacetime army. To any right-thinking person in the late 1930s, it was absurd to suppose that she could ever be defeated in a six-week campaign.

The French military were not unprepared, but they put their faith in the Maginot Line, a state-of-the-art network of bomb- and artillery-proof bunkers, tunnels, and gun emplacements along France's eastern border with Germany and

Luxemburg, which was meant to give the French enough time to mobilize their army in response to an attack from the east. The Maginot Line was effectively impregnable, so Hitler merely went around it, invading through neutral Belgium, whose border with France was unfortified.

Their army routed, their capital occupied, and their leaders forced to sign a humiliating armistice that acquiesced in the occupation of half of the motherland, the French people were in shock. Many conservatives, who largely shared Hitler's aims and anti-Semitic views and approved of his strident anti-Communism, either passively accepted the defeat or actively collaborated with the Vichy regime. But the French Left and those rightwing patriots who refused to accept any surrender, especially to the Germans, began to

organize the Resistance. By 1941, there were eight major resistance organizations in France, separated both by geography and ideology. What was needed was a man of vision and authority who could unite them into a national liberation movement. The man that General de Gaulle chose for this difficult task was Jean Moulin.

Fighting Fascism

Although he had enlisted as soon as he was of age in 1918, Moulin just missed fighting in World War I, as the armistice was signed as he completed his basic training. After the war, he graduated in law and entered the provincial administration. Following French practice, he was posted to prefectures all over France, being made the country's youngest prefect in 1937. He combined his civil service career with a

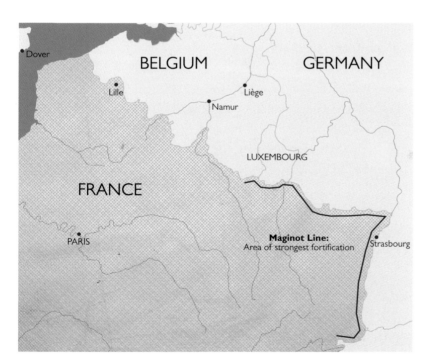

LEFT:
The French had built the defensive Maginot Line on its eastern borders to deter a German attack, but left the border with neutral Belgium unfortified.

FEATURE **Reinventing France**

The *Conseil National de la Résistance* brought together the major Resistance movements, plus representatives of the media, the trade unions, and the underground political parties hostile to the Vichy regime. Jean Moulin was its first president, acting as General de Gaulle's personal representative. Present at the first meeting of the council in Paris on May 27, 1943, were representatives of the eight largest Resistance groups, including the Communist *Franc-Tireurs et Partisans*

Français (FTPF), who had thus far remained aloof from an alliance with the Gaullist Free French. Besides coordinating the military campaign against the Germans, the CNR also produced the blueprint for the governance of postwar France, including the creation of universal social security and pension systems. The creation of the CNR also boosted de Gaulle's position vis-à-vis the Allies, who could no longer doubt that he spoke for the majority of the French people.

political appointment, working for Pierre Cot (1895–1977), who served in several ministerial posts, including as head of the Air Ministry between 1932 and 1940, in a center-left government. Although the French government's official stance during the Spanish Civil War (1936–39) was nonintervention, Cot and Moulin arranged for Russian fighter planes intended for the Spanish Republican forces to be transported across French territory.

The partisan prefect

When France fell, Moulin was prefect of the Eure-et-Loire Department just south of Paris in the German-occupied zone. He had his first brush with the *Gestapo* when he refused to blame French colonial African troops for massacres the Germans had themselves committed. In November 1940, he was dismissed by the Vichy regime, which was purging the provincial administration of anyone who had belonged to parties of the left before the war.

Moulin returned to the family home in the south of France and set himself two tasks: first, to make a complete survey of the French Resistance in Vichy France; and second, to travel to London to begin talks with General de Gaulle, leader of the Free French. Using the fake identity of law professor Joseph Mercier, he traveled across Vichy France to make contact with Resistance leaders.

Having achieved his first aim, he met with de Gaulle in London in September 1941. Although the two men were on opposite sides of the political divide, they recognized in one another a profound patriotism that outweighed their ideological differences. The general appointed Moulin his personal representative, charged with creating a united French Resistance. Once back in France, Moulin established the *Mouvements Unis de la Résistance* in January 1943, which brought together three of the eight major Resistance organizations, and on a subsequent mission in March that year, he succeeded in coopting all eight groups into the *Conseil National de la Résistance* (CNR).

In the hands of the butcher of Lyon

Although the creation of the CNR signaled the success of Moulin's mission, he himself had little time left to enjoy his achievements. A French traitor, who remains unidentified, betrayed Moulin to the *Gestapo* in June 1943. He was arrested while meeting with other resistance leaders in a house in suburban Lyon. He was interrogated by the notorious Klaus Barbie (1913–91), the head of the Lyon *Gestapo*, who

earned the nickname the "butcher of Lyon." Submitted to the most brutal treatment in Lyon and then in Paris, Moulin died while being deported by train to Germany on July 6, 1943.

One of the most celebrated leaders of the French Resistance, his ashes were interred in the Panthéon, the secular mausoleum housing the remains of France's most distinguished sons and daughters.

ABOVE:
The house in Caluire-et-Cuire, Lyon, where Moulin was arrested, along with eight other senior members of the Resistance.

NAME: **Martin Niemöller**

NATIONALITY: German

BIRTH: January 14, 1892
DEATH: March 6, 1984

PROFESSION: Lutheran pastor

CATEGORY: Resistance hero

ACHIEVEMENT: He resisted the Nazi takeover of the Evangelical Church by founding a covenant of dissenting pastors.

A U-boat captain during World War I and a member of the postwar antirevolutionary *Freikorps*, Martin Niemöller was ordained in 1924. An early supporter of Hitler, he later denounced the Nazi takeover of the Evangelical Church and was a central figure in organizing the religious resistance to the Nazis.

If Dietrich Bonhoeffer (pp. 124–127) embodied one type of faith-inspired resistance to Hitler and Nazism, Catholic Bishop Clemens von Galen (pp. 144–147) and the subject of this entry, Lutheran pastor Martin Niemöller, took a quite different journey to arrive at the same destination. Bonhoeffer was liberal to his very core and a committed Christian from his youth. His studies and travels around the world led him to discover and live an ecumenical faith based on the pursuit of social justice. Niemöller's vocation to become a pastor came much later, and was based on a conservative worldview much closer to that of Bishop von Galen and other conservative opponents of the Nazi regime.

Niemöller's conversion to the anti-Nazi cause appears all the more admirable because he had to overcome his deep-seated natural conservatism, but conversely he has been criticized for not speaking out more strongly against the Nazi persecution of the Jews and limiting his criticisms to the Nazi-backed *Deutsche Christen* takeover of the Lutheran Evangelical Church, which he fought with the creation of the Emergency Covenant of Pastors (see Feature, p. 155) and of the Confessing Church (see Feature, p. 126).

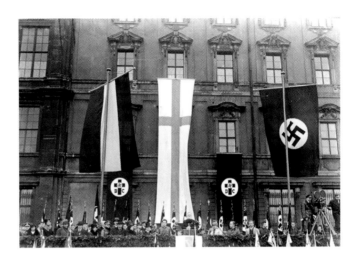

ABOVE:
Members of *Deutsche Christen*, photographed in Berlin in November 1933. Niemöller spoke out against their persecution and subsequent takeover of the Lutheran Evangelical Church.

After the war he strove to make amends for his own perceived failings by being a signatory of the *Stuttgarter Schuldbekenntnis* (Stuttgart Declaration of Guilt; 1945), which admitted that the church had failed to do enough to oppose the Nazis and their genocidal policies. Later in life, he went much further, becoming a convinced pacifist and antimilitarist, and campaigning against the Vietnam War and for nuclear disarmament.

Hero of the high seas

For a man of the cloth, Niemöller did not have the most conventional start to his pastoral career. He was the son of a conservative Lutheran pastor born during the glory days of the Second German Reich, but instead of following in his father's footsteps after high school, he opted to join the Imperial German Navy as an officer cadet. He fought during World War I, serving on ships of the line before being transferred to Germany's formidable U-boat fleet in 1915.

He served with distinction aboard several U-boats in the Mediterranean and Bay of Biscay, where a boat on which he was first officer set a record for the most Allied shipping sunk. In May 1918, he got his own command, the *UC-67*, with which he succeeded in temporarily closing the French port of Marseilles by sinking ships to block the harbor mouth and laying mines in its approaches. His naval service earned an Iron Cross, First Class.

Like many other demobilized German servicemen after World War I, he joined the paramilitary *Freikorps* to combat the uprisings that sought to establish a Soviet-style Communist regime in Germany. In 1919–1920, he was a commander in the Third Münster Defense Battalion, which opposed the leftwing Ruhr Uprising and which later mounted a failed rightwing coup attempt.

From U-boat to pulpit

Niemöller was ordained a pastor of the Lutheran Evangelical Church at the age of 32. He began his church career as a curate in Münster before being appointed as the pastor of a parish in the wealthy Berlin suburb of Dahlem. His change of career, did not, however, reflect a radical shift in political beliefs. He was an early supporter of Hitler and voted for him in the 1924 elections. In the 1930s he supported the idea that Germany needed a strong *Führer* ("guide" or "leader"). In a sermon in 1933, he described the Nazi Party as a "renewal movement based on a Christian moral foundation." His autobiography, *From U-Boat to*

Pulpit, published in 1934, was a hit among Nazi Party members, selling 90,000 copies in the first few weeks after publication.

Breaking with Hitler

Niemöller's disenchantment with Hitler was a slow, drawn-out process, triggered by the Nazi interference in the Evangelical Church. In 1933, he opposed the imposition on the church of the anti-Semitic Aryan Paragraph by founding the *Pfarrernotbund*, and in 1934 he joined Dietrich Bonhoeffer and other Lutheran theologians and pastors in the dissident Confessing Church. Although he opposed Hitler's racist policies, especially when these discriminated against Protestant Christians of Jewish descent, he did not condemn the regime as a whole.

He was arrested in July 1937 and condemned for activities against the state, for which he was fined and served a seven-month prison term. Having been held in detention for longer than his sentence, he was released after his trial, but he was immediately arrested by the *Gestapo* and sent to Sachsenhausen and then Dachau concentration camps, where he remained until 1945. He realized the gravity of his mistake during his imprisonment, and wrote one of most oft-quoted poems about the Nazi wartime persecutions:

In Germany, they came first for the
Communists, And I didn't speak up
because I wasn't a Communist;

And then they came for the trade unionists,
And I didn't speak up because I wasn't a
trade unionist;

And then they came for the Jews, And I
didn't speak up because I wasn't a Jew;

And then … they came for me … And by
that time there was no one left to speak up.

FEATURE | **Anti-Nazi covenant**

In the elections to Church offices held in July 1933, after Hitler's election as Reich chancellor, the Nazi-backed *Deutsche Christen* movement won a majority in all but four provinces of the Evangelical Church, aligning the churches closely with the aims and ideology of the Nazi Party. Central to the Nazi program at this time was the introduction of the Aryan Paragraph, which excluded Jews and Christians of Jewish descent from participating in civil society. The pro-Nazi leaders of the Evangelical Church adopted the Aryan Paragraph, causing a schism between the "destroyed" and "intact" churches. Martin Niemöller countered by establishing the *Pfarrernotbund* (Emergency Covenant of Pastors) to oppose the introduction of the Aryan Paragraph and the Nazi attempt to merge the Evangelical churches into a single Reich Church that would stress Nazi ideology over Jewish and Christian values. At its height the covenant was signed by over 7,000 members and pastors of the Church.

NAME:	**Hotsumi Ozaki**
NATIONALITY:	Japanese
BIRTH:	April 29, 1901
DEATH:	November 7, 1944
PROFESSION:	Journalist and Soviet spy
CATEGORY:	Resistance hero
ACHIEVEMENT:	An agent of the Sorge spy network, he provided crucial information that helped Russia defeat Germany.

A convert to Communism while he was a student, Hotsumi Ozaki became a journalist specializing in Sino-Japanese relations. While working in China, he was recruited by Soviet spymaster Richard Sorge. Back in Japan, Ozaki became a senior government adviser, and thus was one of Russian Intelligence's most valuable assets in Tokyo.

Anyone who has lived, studied, and worked in Japan may be surprised that a prewar Japanese "subject"—as the Japanese only became "citizens" in the postwar period—could ever betray his emperor and country, and by extension his family and culture. Of course, that is not to say that there were no committed opponents of the Japanese governments that took the empire to war against China in 1937 and against the USA

and the British Empire in 1941, but opposition is not the same as betrayal.

Those familiar with Japanese society, education, religion, and family life—even in their liberal-democratic postwar manifestations—will understand why Hotsumi Ozaki was the only Japanese to be executed for treason during World War II; and why many leftwing opponents of the imperial government performed *tenkō*—literally, "about face"—renouncing their former political allegiances and returning to the imperial fold. A Japanese proverb captures the prevailing sentiment at that time: "The nail that sticks out will be hammered down."

China expert

If we are to explain why Ozaki was one of the few Japanese who betrayed his homeland by spying for an enemy country during the war, we could start by examining his upbringing and education. He grew up in Taipei, now capital of Taiwan, then a Japanese colony, where his father worked as a newspaper editor. This exposed him to the discriminatory attitudes of the majority of prewar Japanese vis-à-vis other Asians, and in particular their Chinese and Korean colonial subjects. A year later he returned to Japan to study law, and witnessed the mob-led massacres of Koreans accused of sabotage and well-poisoning after the Great Kantō Earthquake of 1923. The violence was often carried out with the collusion of the police and army. Disgusted, he became a Marxist, joining the Communist Party in 1925. In 1926 he started work for the *Asahi Shimbun* newspaper in Tokyo and then Osaka. From 1928, he was posted to Shanghai as the paper's China correspondent. In China he met members of the Communist Party and was introduced to Richard Sorge (pp. 94–97), who recruited him to the GRU (see Feature, p. 97).

Advising the prime minister

Once back in Japan, and on the strength of his reputation as a China expert, Ozaki was invited to join a think tank established by Prime Minister Fumimaro Konoe (1891–1945). This gave him and his boss Sorge unrivaled access to the inner workings of the Japanese government, and allowed Ozaki to influence important policy decisions. He advised against a Japanese invasion of Siberia, and was able to confirm to Sorge that the Japanese would not attack the Soviet Far East in 1941, as Hitler had repeatedly requested. The information, once relayed to Moscow, helped ensure Hitler's defeat in the European war. When Sorge was arrested and tortured, he revealed his entire network of spies, including Ozaki, who was condemned to death for treason and hanged on November 7, 1944.

NAME: **Gilbert Renault**

NATIONALITY: French

BIRTH: August 6, 1904

DEATH: July 29, 1984

PROFESSION: Member of the French Resistance

CATEGORY: Resistance hero

ACHIEVEMENT: He took over and ran one of the most important French wartime information networks.

A member of an ultranationalist Catholic monarchist party of the prewar French extreme right, Gilbert Renault refused to collaborate with the Vichy regime and chose to join the Free French under General de Gaulle. He helped organize and run one of wartime France's largest information networks, the *Confrérie Notre-Dame*.

The French Third Republic, like many other European governments between the two world wars, was deeply divided along political lines, with parties of the extreme left and right attempting to subvert and destabilize a succession of center-right or center-left coalition governments. The members of one party of the French extreme right, the royalist, ultra-Catholic *Action Française* (AF), who should have been sympathetic to Hitler as they shared his anti-Semitic views, in fact opposed him because their ultranationalist credo defined a resurgent Germany as the main existential threat to France.

After France was defeated, the supporters of the movement fell into three broad groups: the first, like AF leader Charles Maurras (1868–1952), gave grudging support but not full cooperation to the Pétain regime, in the name of national unity; the second collaborated wholeheartedly with Vichy and the Germans; and the third, like Gilbert Renault, also known by a number of wartime codenames and aliases, the most famous of which was "Colonel Rémy," opted for out-and-out resistance, both to the Vichy puppet state and the German occupation. But in joining the Free French under de Gaulle, Renault had to accept that he would be fighting alongside bitter prewar political rivals of the left and extreme left.

For God and king

Renault was the eldest of nine children born to a conservative Catholic family from Brittany, an area traditionally associated with French monarchism. He graduated from a Catholic high school run by the Jesuit teaching order before studying law at the University of Rennes. His first job was with the Banque de France, which he joined in 1924, but in 1936, he became a film producer, financing a movie by rightwing and later pro-Vichy film director Abel Gance (1889–1981). From his student days Renault had been a supporter of *Action Française*, taking part in riots in Paris in February 1934, from which he returned with "his clothes spattered with mud and ... a black eye."

ABOVE:
German soldiers in conversation with Parisians in June 1940. Renault was not as accommodating to the German occupiers and their Vichy collaborators.

When Marshal Pétain signed the armistice with Hitler, Renault did not hesitate to reject what he saw as a betrayal of France, later explaining his decision thus: "As a supporter of *Action Française*, I could not accept that France had been so definitively beaten." On June 18, the day General de Gaulle made his appeal to the French people, Renault, accompanied by one of his younger brothers, traveled to England.

Fighting for Our Lady

Once in England he presented himself at de Gaulle's London HQ, where he was assigned to André Dewavrin's (pp. 140–143) BCRA as an intelligence officer. The Free French intelligence chief tasked him with setting up an information network in France. Renault slipped back into Vichy France via

Map labels: Dover, Dunkirk, Lille, PARIS, Strasbourg, **OCCUPIED ZONE**, La Rochelle, Angoulême, VICHY, Lyon, Le Verdon, Pauillac, Grenoble, Bordeaux, Saint-Antoine-de-Breuilh, **VICHY FREE ZONE**, Bayonne, Pau, Toulouse, Nice, Marseilles, Toulon, Laruns

ABOVE:
After its defeat, France was divided into the German-occupied north and west, and the Vichy-controlled south, bordering on neutral Switzerland and Axis Italy.

Spain. He joined forces with another rightwing recruit to the French Resistance, Louis de La Bardonnie (1902–87), who had already set up an information network based in the Dordogne village of Saint-Antoine-de-Breuilh.

The network, which under Renault's guidance took the very Catholic name of the *Confrérie Notre-Dame* (CND; Brotherhood of Our Lady), became one of the largest Resistance intelligence-gathering organizations in France, with 1,375 agents working from stations in La Rochelle, Angoulême, Bordeaux, Le Verdon, Pauillac, Bayonne, Pau, Laruns, Toulouse, and Vichy, spanning both sides of the border between the occupied German zone and Vichy France, and operating safe crossing points and letterboxes for Resistance fighters and SOE agents on both sides of the line.

The group's first radio transmitter was installed at de La Bardonnie's Château de La Roque in February 1941 and went into service one month later. Among the successes attributed to information provided by CND agents were the sinking of the German flagship, the *Bismarck*, in May 1941, the blockading of the battlecruisers *Scharnhost* and *Gneisenau* in the port of Brest, and the successful British raid on the Bruneval Würzburg station (see Feature, opposite).

Old enemies, new friends

In June 1942, Renault traveled back to France, but, tracked by *Gestapo* agents, he was forced to return to England aboard a fishing boat. Nevertheless, he carried with him a German map of the West Wall, a detailed plan of the coastal defenses of Normandy, which would be a key piece of intelligence used in the planning of Operation Overlord. In 1943, Renault returned to France and with the help of Socialist Resistance leader, Pierre Brossolette (pp. 132–135), established the first contacts between the Free French and the Communist *Franc-Tireurs et Partisans* Resistance group, taking the Communist Party's spokesperson Fernand Grenier (1901–92) back to London to meet de Gaulle. In November that year, the CND was betrayed by one of its agents and much of the network was dismantled by German counterintelligence. Despite these serious losses and the arrest of de La Bardonnie, Renault supervised the creation of a new network codenamed "Castille."

His final wartime mission took place during the liberation of Paris in August 1944, when he headed a group of 60 commandos, with orders to seize the Majestic Hotel and secure the German occupation archives.

ABOVE:
British forces pictured in training for the 1942 raid on the Würzburg station at Bruneval. CND information was crucial to the success of the operation.

FEATURE **Putting the bite on German radar**

In the entry on Reginald Jones (pp. 20–23), I explained how the British managed to stay one step ahead of the German aircraft guidance systems by combining Enigma decrypts with the analysis of captured equipment from downed enemy aircraft. When the British began their own bombing campaign against German cities, they initially sustained heavy losses. Jones used RAF reconnaissance photographs and reports from Renault's CND to identify German Würzburg radar installations in occupied France. Given the name

Operation Biting, British forces targeted an isolated Würzburg station on the French Atlantic coast near the village of Bruneval. Because the station was protected by strong coastal defenses, a commando unit was parachuted in on the night of February 27–28, 1942. Thanks to CND intelligence, the raid was a resounding success. The unit returned to England by landing craft, taking with them key parts of the Würzburg system, as well as the station's operators.

NAME: **Sophie Scholl**

NATIONALITY: German

BIRTH: May 9, 1921
DEATH: February 22, 1943

PROFESSION: University student

CATEGORY: Resistance hero

ACHIEVEMENT: A member of a nonviolent German resistance group based in Munich.

Sophie Scholl was an ordinary German student from a liberal Christian family. She became so disgusted with the Nazis that she joined her brother and other students from the University of Munich in distributing anti-regime pamphlets, advocating passive nonviolent resistance. Caught distributing the group's sixth pamphlet, she was tried and executed.

There comes a time in the lifecycle of every dictatorship when its members have so lost touch with reality and their own humanity that they start to devour their own children. In Nazi Germany, this happened in February 1943, when a German People's Court condemned three college students to death for treason, not for throwing Molotov cocktails, building barricades, or murdering police officers, but for no other crime other than expressing opposition to Nazi policies and advocating passive resistance by distributing pamphlets.

An ordinary schoolgirl
Sophie Scholl's early life in Weimar Germany is so unremarkable that it is difficult to understand why a Lutheran schoolgirl from the small town of Forchtenberg in the southwestern state of

Baden-Württemberg met her end on the guillotine at the age of 22. She was the daughter of Christian-Democratic politician Robert Scholl (1891–1973), who was imprisoned by the Nazis for calling Hitler a "scourge of God." Despite her parents' liberal views, Sophie joined the *Bund Deutscher Mädel* (League of German Girls), the female equivalent of the Hitler Youth.

In 1941, after graduating from high school and as a precondition for going to college, she had to serve 6 months in the *Reichsarbeitsdienst* (National Labor Service). Her experiences in two Nazi organizations and during her first year at the University of Munich, where she joined her elder brother Hans (1918–1943), made her reconsider the stance an individual should adopt under a dictatorship.

Blood rose

After reading a sermon by Bishop von Galen (pp. 144–147) and hearing eyewitness accounts of the atrocities committed by German troops on the Eastern Front, Sophie, Hans, and several of their student friends formed a resistance group called *die Weiße Rose* (the White Rose). They produced a total of six pamphlets, listing the crimes of the Nazi regime and advocating nonviolent resistance. The pamphlets were left in public phone booths and taken by couriers to be mailed in other cities. They targeted people they believed would be more likely to share their views, such as intellectuals, university professors, and students. Using the simple duplicating technology of the day, they managed to produce between 6,000 and 9,000 copies of their fifth pamphlet. At the same time the group carried out a graffiti campaign on university buildings and Munich landmarks, where they stenciled the slogans, "Down with Hitler" and "Freedom."

ABOVE:
Christoph Probst, member of the White Rose resistance group, photographed around 1940.

On February 18, 1943, Hans and Sophie were leaving pamphlets around the University of Munich when they were seen by a janitor, who called the *Gestapo*. Although they tried to shield their friends, they had material on them implicating other members of the White Rose, who were quickly arrested and tried for treason. After the briefest of hearings, Hans, Sophie, and Christoph Probst (1918–43; pictured above), were found guilty and sentenced to death by beheading on the guillotine.

NAME: Ariadna Scriabina

NATIONALITY: Russian

BIRTH: October 26, 1905

DEATH: July 22, 1944

PROFESSION: Resistance fighter

CATEGORY: Resistance hero

ACHIEVEMENT: She was an organizer and active member of the armed Jewish resistance in France.

The daughter of Russian composer Alexander Scriabin, Ariadna Scriabina moved to Paris in 1922. She converted to Judaism when she married her third husband. After the fall of France, she was a founding member of the French Jewish armed resistance organization, the *Armée Juive*, which fought against the Germans and Vichy regime.

There are some people whose lives read as if they have been lifted out of a work of fiction. One such is Russian exile Ariadna Scriabina, unconventional hard-drinking Bohemian poet and hero of the French Jewish armed resistance, whose biography could have been penned by fellow Russian writer Boris Pasternak (1890–1960). Born in 1905, Scriabina shared many of the experiences of the protagonists of

Dr. Zhivago (1957), Pasternak's famous novel about World War I and the events of the Russian Revolution.

Our view of the pre-1939 Soviet Union is colored by the excesses of the Stalinist 1930s and the decades of the Cold War following Stalin's death in 1953, but Russia between 1917 and the death of Lenin (1870–1924) was not the oppressive one-party state it was destined to become. For a brief period, as the repression of the previous Czarist regime lifted and before Communist totalitarianism took hold, Soviet society flowered as a bold experiment in socialism, egalitarianism, and modernism. It became a haven for artistic, political, social, and sexual dissidents from all over the world. It was in this heady atmosphere of hope for a more just society, which was constantly under threat from civil war, foreign invasion, political extremism, and economic disaster, that Scriabina grew up and acquired her worldview.

Daughter of a famous father

Ariadna was the eldest of three children born to Tatiana Schletzer and Alexander Scriabin (1872–1915), who already had four children with his legitimate wife Vera Scriabina. Ariadna was born in Italy, where Scriabin was working on *The Poem of Ecstasy* (1905–08). Constantly short of funds and obliged to take on concert tours, the Scriabin-Schletzer household traveled all over Europe, settling briefly in Amsterdam, Paris, Brussels, Geneva, and Lausanne. Scriabin's unconventional family life kept him out of Russia until 1909, but when he returned to Moscow, he had his three children baptized into the Russian Orthodox Church.

In Moscow, Scriabin entertained artists, poets, actors, and intellectuals, who influenced Ariadna and her siblings to pursue artistic careers. She attended the Moscow Conservatoire and wrote poetry. Scriabin died suddenly of septicemia in 1915, leaving his family without support.

ABOVE:
The three Scriabin-Schletzer children (from left to right): Julian, Marina, and Ariadna.

LEFT:
Raised in the Bohemian world of artists, writers, and musicians, the young Ariadna (left) wanted to be a famous poet in her own right.

Magnanimously, Vera recognized Ariadna and her siblings as her husband's children, allowing them to use their father's name.

To the City of Lights

In 1922, after several difficult years in Russia, which saw the death of her mother and younger brother, Ariadna went to Paris to join her uncle, Boris Schletzer. Frequenting the city's large Russian émigré community, she was determined to become a famous poet. She was married twice, the first time in 1924 to French composer Daniel Lazarus, who admired her unconventional ways;

and the second, to French writer René Méjean. In 1934, she fell in love with restaurant owner, aspiring poet, and Zionist activist Dovid Knut (1900–55), a Jew from Bessarabia, a part of the Russian Empire that had been annexed by Romania.

The pair needed to divorce their respective spouses before they could marry, which Knut did in 1933 and Ariadna in 1937. The couple married at the beginning of 1939. It is typical of Ariadna that not only did she choose to marry a Jew at a time when his co-religionists were being persecuted all over Europe, but she also converted to Judaism, adopting the name Sarah. The pair were ardent Zionists, which in Ariadna's case sometimes shaded into an intolerance that even shocked her Jewish friends. For example, after a visit to British Mandatory Palestine in 1937, she declared: "The only two solutions to the Arab problem are to drive them out or slit their throats."

Que faire?

Drafted into the French army in 1939, Knut found himself in the southern city of Toulouse when France surrendered. Ariadna moved from Paris to join him in the city, which was in Vichy France and therefore marginally less dangerous to France's Jews than the German-occupied north and west. Nevertheless Ariadna and Knut stopped speaking Russian for fear of being denounced as Jews to the Vichy-sponsored *Milice Française* (French Militia).

FEATURE **Taking a strong hand**

After the rout of the French army in May 1940, French Jews realized the precariousness of their situation in a country half of which was occupied by the Nazis, while the other was governed by an anti-Semitic German-sponsored regime. In Toulouse, Abraham Polonski, Ariadna, and Dovid Knut, and several of their Zionist friends, created the *Main Forte* (Strong Hand) group to help Jews interned in local concentration camps. In 1942, the group became the armed resistance movement, the *Armée Juive* (AJ). At its height, the AJ consisted of more than 2,000 fighters, who helped Jews from across occupied Europe escape across the Pyrenees into neutral Spain, from where they traveled to Mandatory Palestine. In February 1943, the AJ recruited former army officer Jacques Lazarus (1916–2014) to train its fighters, who went on the offensive against the Vichy *Milice* and the Germans and targeted collaborators who denounced Jews.

At the beginning of 1942, Knut and Ariadna circulated an underground pamphlet entitled *Que Faire?* (*What Should We Do?*), which discussed the plight of the Jews, arguing that they should set up a Jewish resistance organization. Although most of their Jewish friends considered the idea to be tantamount to suicide, the couple won the support of Polish-born engineer Abraham Polonski (born ca.1903), with whom they founded the *Armée Juive*, or AJ (see Feature, opposite). Ariadna's main role in the AJ was to organize the rescue of orphaned Jewish children and help them to escape to neutral countries.

In December 1942, after the arrest and torture of one of the AJ's members, Knut was forced to flee to Switzerland, but Ariadna stayed on in Toulouse. In July 1944, two weeks before the liberation of the city, Ariadna was caught in a militia ambush and shot in the ensuing firefight.

ABOVE:
Ariadna with her third husband, Dovid Knut, who was a Bessarabian Jew. He survived the war, while she was gunned down in a militia ambush.

NAME: **Claus von Stauffenberg**

NATIONALITY: German

BIRTH: November 15, 1907

DEATH: July 21, 1944

PROFESSION: *Wehrmacht* officer

CATEGORY: Resistance hero

ACHIEVEMENT: He plotted to overthrow Hitler, and was one of the main movers behind the July 20 plot on Hitler's life.

The scion of an illustrious noble house, Claus von Stauffenberg climbed through the ranks to become a colonel in the *Werhmacht*, serving in all the major campaigns of the war. Disillusioned with Hitler, he was one of the main conspirators who plotted the last attempt on the dictator's life.

Novelists and historians are fond of what-if scenarios, and among two of the most popular for this period are: "What if Germanu had won World War II?" and "What if Hitler had been assassinated during the war?" The first need not delay us long, because after the stalled Russian offensive and Knut Haukelid's daring raid that denied Hitler the atomic bomb (see pp. 62–65), it was clear to the military strategists on both sides that Germany had lost the war. But the second offers much more intriguing possibilities: How would the Allies have dealt with a scenario in which Hitler and the Nazi leadership were dead or in prison and the SS, SD, and *Gestapo* liquidated, but the German army, air force, and navy remained mostly intact? What challenges would have been posed by a country that was still a military force?

This question exercised the minds of the members of the *Schwarze Kapelle* (Black Orchestra; see Feature, p. 170), the name given by the *Gestapo* to the conservative German resistance in an echo of Leopold Trepper's (pp. 102–105) Soviet-backed spy network, the *Rote Kapelle*, the Red Orchestra. The threat from the Black Orchestra, which included members drawn from the highest ranks of the armed forces, was by far the greater, and von Stauffenberg, as one of the main instigators of the July 20 plot, remains one of its best-known leaders. While he is hailed as a hero of the German resistance, several historians have questioned his motives, claiming that, had von Stauffenberg been successful and gone on to shape the country's future course, a post-Hitler Germany would have remained aggressively militaristic and National Socialist in all but name.

ABOVE:
Hitler at the Wolf's Lair, his forward headquarters in East Prussia (now Poland), where von Stauffenberg (pictured here, farthest left) carried out his assassination attempt on July 20, 1944.

The Swabian count

Claus von Stauffenberg had the perfect pedigree, background, and education to have become a grandee of the First and Second German Reich. His family had served Germany's titular Holy Roman emperors since the 13th century, and his father had been a high court official of the Kingdom of Württemberg before German unification. Sadly for him, he grew up during the Weimar Republic, which had abolished the titles and privileges of the old imperial aristocracy. But unlike French aristocrats, who lost their power, titles, and land, along with their heads, during the French Revolution of 1789, the German Junkers kept their wealth and landed estates, and though without constitutional power, wielded a great deal of influence. Count von Stauffenberg had the boundless self-confidence of a member of a former ruling elite, whose self-importance was bolstered by seven centuries of privilege, wealth, and tradition.

FEATURE **Facing the music**

The *Schwarze Kapelle* (Black Orchestra) is the name given to the conservative military resistance to Hitler between 1938 and 1944. The *Schwarze Kapelle* was not a single network but consisted of several groups of men from the higher echelons of the armed forces, who knew one another and shared broadly similar objectives. Many, such as Ludwig Beck (pp. 120–123) and Wilhelm Canaris (pp. 136–139) had served in World War I, and were convinced that Hitler's invasion of Czechoslovakia and Poland would lead to a second German defeat and humiliation, and a further scaling back of the armed forces. Their aim was to overthrow Hitler in a military coup, and sign a peace with the Allies that would allow Germany to keep its territorial gains in central and eastern Europe. As Hitler began to lose the war, the military plots and assassination attempts multiplied, but the Führer survived them all unscathed, until he was wounded in their final attempt in the July 20 plot.

In the brave new world of the Weimar democracy, the only possible destination for a young man of his class was the armed forces. He joined the family's cavalry regiment in 1926 and received his lieutenant's commission in 1930. His commanding officer, General Erich Hoepner (1886–1944) was one of the plotters who hoped to topple Hitler during the Munich Crisis of 1938. Although von Stauffenberg remained loyal to Hitler until 1943, like Beck and Canaris, he had enough reservations not to join the Nazi Party. Although himself a militarist and an anti-Semite, as a practicing Catholic von Stauffenberg objected to the ill-treatment of the Jews, and as a career soldier he feared that Hitler's military adventurism would lead to defeat and a second German humiliation.

The low road to high treason

For a man like von Stauffenberg, the thought of breaking his soldier's oath and rebelling against his commander-in-chief was, at first, unthinkable, and his conversion from loyal officer to would-be assassin was a slow process. He served in the victorious campaigns in Poland and France, attributing their success to Hitler's leadership. This opinion of Hitler began to change, however, during the invasion of Russia, where he was shocked by German atrocities against Jews and Russian POWs. During the failed counter-offensive against the Allied invasion of North Africa, he was seriously wounded, losing one eye, his right hand, and two fingers on his left hand.

LEFT:
The wrecked conference room where von Stauffenberg had planted the bomb. Hitler was protected from serious injury by a heavy oak table.

The three-fingered assassin

It would be difficult to say how much von Stauffenberg's injuries played a part in his decision to join the German resistance, but often personal misfortune combines with external events to push an individual to a radical rethink of his or her worldview. After several aborted or failed coup attempts in 1943, and with the Allied beachhead established in Normandy in June 1944, von Stauffenberg decided to take matters into his own hands. He still hoped, though by then unrealistically, that the Allies would grant Germany a conditional surrender, if Hitler could be removed.

On July 20, 1944, von Stauffenberg got his chance when he was summoned to attend a conference at the *Wolfsschanze*—the Wolf's Lair—Hitler's forward HQ in Poland. Although the venue was changed at the last minute, von Stauffenberg managed to plant a briefcase containing a bomb under the conference table. He left the room minutes before the bomb went off. Convinced that Hitler and his senior staff had been killed in the blast, he flew back to Berlin to stage a military coup against the decapitated Nazi regime. Although injured, Hitler had been protected from the worst of the explosion by the heavy oak table. Among the first plotters to be arrested, von Stauffenberg and three other conspirators were court-martialed and executed by firing squad the next day.

NAME: **Adam von Trott zu Solz**

NATIONALITY: German

BIRTH: August 9, 1909
DEATH: August 26, 1944

PROFESSION: Diplomat and lawyer

CATEGORY: Resistance hero

ACHIEVEMENT: A member of the conservative opposition to Hitler, he plotted to overthrow the Nazi regime.

Although from a similar aristocratic, conservative background to many of the military plotters in the Black Orchestra resistance movement, Adam von Trott zu Solz had quite different motives from his fellow conspirators. A lawyer and diplomat, he was an internationalist and Christian, who opposed the Nazis on moral grounds.

Adam von Trott zu Solz represents a third group within the conservative opposition to Hitler, alongside the military and the Churches. An aristocrat and a committed Christian, he was also an urbane internationalist. During the "Roaring Twenties," the Weimar Republic was probably one of the most forward-looking nations in the world. Anyone who has read Christopher Isherwood's *Goodbye to Berlin* (1939) or seen its screen adaptation, *Cabaret* (1972), will get a flavor of the striking political contrasts that existed in prewar Germany between the "divinely decadent" (to quote Sally Bowles, aka Liza Minnelli [b. 1946]) bohemians and upper classes and the deeply conservative, Christian working and middle classes.

Many of the conservatives who had supported Hitler as a bulwark against Communism woke up far too late to the threat that he posed to their own power and to the future of Germany. After the establishment of the one-party Nazi dictatorship in 1934, the only option left to the conservative opposition was regime change.

Man of the world

Unlike fellow Black Orchestra plotters Ludwig Beck (pp. 120–123) and Wilhelm Canaris (pp. 136–139), von Trott was too young to have fought in World War I, and though he no doubt felt the humiliation of the Treaty of Versailles, he was not personally implicated in Germany's defeat. He was of the same generation as Claus von Stauffenberg, but his motivations for joining the opposition were very different from those of his military peers.

While a student, he spent a term at Oxford University in 1929, returning on a two-year Rhodes Scholarship in 1931. When he went back to Germany in 1933, he opted to join the legal profession, but was hampered in his career by his opposition to the Nazis, his refusal to join the Party, and his choice of a Jewish law firm for his internship. Facing continuing discrimination, he left Germany, obtaining a third-year Rhodes scholarship to study in China. He later spent time in the USA and UK, establishing contacts with British and American politicians and intellectuals.

Like Canaris, von Trott thought that he could best oppose the regime from within. On his return to Berlin in 1940, he accepted an invitation to join the foreign service. The post gave him access to the Nazis' plans and allowed him to travel freely to neutral countries, where he contacted Allied agents to inform them of the activities of the resistance and attempted to negotiate favorable terms should a coup succeed in removing Hitler. In 1943, the Allies announced that they would only accept an unconditional German surrender. Undeterred, von Trott visited von Stauffenberg in Berlin on July 19, 1944, and encouraged him to carry out his assassination attempt the following day. As the plot unraveled, von Trott was arrested and put on trial. He was condemned to death for high treason on August 15 and hanged on August 26.

ABOVE:

Identified as a member of the Black Orchestra and implicated in the July 20 plot, von Trott was executed with the other conspirators.

SECTION: # Escape heroes

MISSION: In this final section of *Secret Heroes of World War II*, two very different categories of "escape artist" are featured. The first applies to those who managed to get out of supposedly escape-proof concentration camps, *Stalags*, and *Oflags* of the Third Reich—people, in other words, that no prison could hold. The second group, however, contains those whose stories are arguably the most admirable and moving. Though the danger these individuals faced was perhaps not quite so perilous, this second category of people were those who risked their reputations, their wealth, their lives, and the lives of their loved ones to help those unfortunates faced with Nazi oppression, violence, and murder.

NAME: Douglas Bader

NATIONALITY: British

BIRTH: February 21, 1910

DEATH: September 5, 1982

PROFESSION: RAF pilot

CATEGORY: Escape hero

ACHIEVEMENT: Shot down over occupied France and captured, he made repeated attempts to escape.

A World War II flying ace with many enemy kills to his name, Douglas Bader is noteworthy because he flew and fought without his legs, which he had lost in a prewar flying accident. Shot down and captured, he made repeated attempts to escape, until interned in Colditz Castle POW camp.

As has been evident thus far, the scale of the secret war fought alongside the battlefield campaigns was impressive. It was a shadow war, waged by secret agents, counterintelligence officers, collaborators, and resistance fighters, which was far from clean or honorable, because it was not governed by the principles of the Hague or Geneva Conventions (1907 and 1929 respectively) on the treatments of military prisoners of war. But even when it comes to the history of World War II, we can identify a second, quite different, secret war: The one fought by Allied POWs, who felt it their sworn duty to escape from detention to return to the fight. Because these were military prisoners, under military jurisdiction, they were usually accorded reasonable treatment and living conditions, even when they tried to escape and were recaptured. Hence alongside the horror of the mass deportations and murders of Jews and the torture and summary execution of SOE agents and resistance fighters, we have stories of derring-do by brave British and French soldiers, who never tired of "goon-bating," that is, making their German captors' lives as miserable as possible, by planning extraordinary and sometimes preposterous escapes.

There is one major exception to this rosy picture of war as one big adventure: The POWs of Slav, Polish, and Russian origin were treated with appalling brutality. They were starved, worked to death, used in sickening medical experiments, tortured, and summarily executed, because the Germans considered them to be "sub-human" and therefore, like the Jews, not protected by the norms of civilized behavior and the laws of war set up to regulate the treatment of military and civilian prisoners.

Bad show

Ill-disciplined, unloved, and neglected as a child, Douglas Bader thrived in the competitive, rough-and-tumble atmosphere of a minor British public (ie, private, fee-based) school, where he excelled at most sports. His rebellious streak continued to get him into trouble when he joined the RAF as an officer cadet, but he completed his training and was commissioned a pilot officer in July 1930. In 1931, on a visit to Reading Aero Club near London, he crashed his plane while attempting some low-flying, daredevil stunts. Seriously injured and fortunate to have survived, he had to have both his legs amputated, one above the knee and one below. His only comment after the accident was: "Crashed slow-rolling near ground. Bad show."

BELOW:
Despite a flying accident in which he lost both legs before the war, Bader taught himself to fly again and persuaded the RAF to take him back.

Although Bader made an extraordinary recovery, learning to drive and fly with his prosthetic legs, the RAF did not consider him fit enough for active duty until the fall of 1939, when after persistent efforts, he regained his wings and was allowed to fly solo again after a break of eight years. Flying Hawker Hurricanes and Supermarine Spitfires (see Reginald Mitchell, pp. 24–27), he took part in the Battles of France

and Britain (1940) and, in the summer of 1941, in the Allied bombing campaign over northwestern Europe. He achieved an impressive number of kills of enemy fighters and bombers and earned a promotion to wing commander.

On August 9, under circumstances that are still not well understood, his Spitfire was hit over northern France. When bailing out, Bader was forced to abandon his right prosthetic leg that had got trapped in the cockpit. Such was the respect that he inspired among the pilots of the *Luftwaffe* that Reichsmarschall Hermann Göring (1893–1946) personally allowed Bader's squadron to fly over the port of St. Omer unopposed to drop a replacement prosthesis for him by parachute.

No leg to stand on

Bader did not waste time before trying to escape, obtaining the help of a member of the cleaning staff of the hospital in St. Omer where he was convalescing. He knotted bed sheets together, removing one from under a comatose patient who had just had his arm amputated, to make an improvised rope and climb down from the window of the hospital ward. He made his way to a safe house outside the town, where he waited for a British agent, who was to smuggle him back to Britain. On this occasion, a French collaborator working in the hospital foiled Bader's escape attempt. He hid from the German search party in a garden but was recaptured a few hours later. His French accomplices were arrested and deported to labor camps in Germany.

Once fully recovered, Bader made so many escape attempts that the Germans threatened to take away his prosthetic legs. He was transferred to *Stalag Luft III*, an air force-run camp that would be the site of the ill-fated "Great Escape" of 76 prisoners in March 1943. Bader was more fortunate when, seven months earlier, he succeeded in escaping with three other inmates. On this occasion his fame betrayed him and led to his recapture. A German fighter pilot, who was visiting the camp and wanted to meet

Bader, found that he was missing and raised the alarm. Bader was apprehended a few days later. As a repeat offender, he was sent to the "escape-proof" Colditz Castle, *Oflag IV-C* (see Feature, below), where he remained until the castle was liberated by U.S. forces on April 15, 1945.

LEFT AND ABOVE:
Two views of Coldtiz Castle, to which Allied soldiers with the escape habit were sent. Despite its heightened security, it had the worst record for attempted and successful escapes.

FEATURE **Hitler's Alcatraz**

Schloss Colditz is a Renaissance castle, built on a spur overlooking the small town of Colditz on the River Mulde, which is a 31-mile (50km) drive from Leipzig in the State of Saxony. During the war it was *Werhmacht Oflag* (Officer's Camp) *IV-C*, which was reserved for the most troublesome prisoners who had repeatedly tried to escape from less secure *Stalag* POW camps. The large outer court, the Kommandantur, housed the German garrison, and the adjacent inner court was

home to the detainees. Despite its forbidding position and the elaborate security measures the Germans had put in place, it had the worst record for attempted and successful escapes. One of the most daring escapes, which was sadly never executed, involved a plan to use a glider, the *Colditz Cock*, that the prisoners built in secret in the attics a few months before the liberation of the castle.

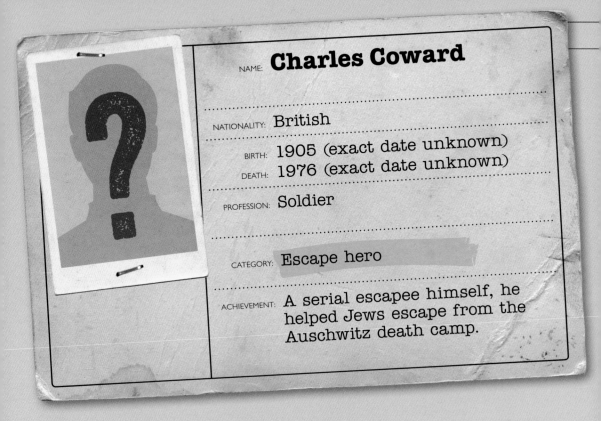

NAME: **Charles Coward**

NATIONALITY: British

BIRTH: 1905 (exact date unknown)

DEATH: 1976 (exact date unknown)

PROFESSION: Soldier

CATEGORY: Escape hero

ACHIEVEMENT: A serial escapee himself, he helped Jews escape from the Auschwitz death camp.

Nicknamed the "Count of Auschwitz" because he helped Jewish inmates of the notorious death camp to escape the gas chambers when they were marched out on slave labor details at the nearby IG Farben works, Charles Coward was himself a serial escapee from German POW camps.

Of the two types of Escape hero outlined in the introduction to this section, Charles Coward could reasonably be placed in both. He was initially detained as a POW in northern France and escaped on at least nine occasions before helping Jewish inmates escape from the Auschwitz-Birkenau death camp. Although there is no agreement as to the exact number of Jewish lives he saved, he earned a place in the company of the "Righteous Among the Nations," commemorated in the "Avenue of Righteous Gentiles" at the Holocaust Memorial of *Yad Vashem* in Jerusalem.

A slippery customer

Charles Coward's wartime exploits were so extraordinary that they became the subject of a book, *The Password Is Courage* (1954), which was made into a movie starring Dirk Bogarde (1921–99) in 1962. Coward began the war like many other British servicemen, serving in France, with the rank of sergeant major. He was taken prisoner near Calais but proved a difficult man to keep interned, managing two escapes before he saw the inside of his first POW camp. During one of his subsequent seven escapes, he hid in a *Wehrmacht* field hospital, passing himself off as a wounded German soldier, and was awarded the Iron Cross for his imaginary services to the Reich.

Throughout his captivity he wrote letters to England addressed to his father, who was, in fact, deceased, care of a "Mr. William Orange," his codename for the real intended recipient: the War Office in London. In the letters he provided information on military movements, the conditions of inmates of POW camps, and, once he had been interned in a camp near the Polish town of Oświęcim, better known as Auschwitz, estimates of the number of Jews arriving by train from different European countries.

Dead men walking

In December 1943, Coward was transferred to the Auschwitz III-Monowitz labor camp, which was 5 miles (8km) from the Auschwitz II-Birkenau death camp. Thanks to his position as Red Cross liaison officer in charge of the welfare of the British POWs at Monowitz, he could move freely within the camp and the surrounding area.

By using Red Cross supplies intended for British POWs, in particular chocolate that was impossible to get in Germany, he bought the corpses of non-Jewish prisoners from the camp's SS guards. He planted the bodies along the route from Monowitz to Birkenau taken by Jewish slave laborers considered too weak to work and destined for the gas chambers, instructing them to drop out and hide at given locations. When the guards counted the prisoners, they included the planted corpses in the tally. The rescued Jews were given the papers of the dead men and smuggled out of the camp.

ABOVE:
The Nazis operated different kinds of internment and extermination camps: the death camps, used to implement the "Final Solution," and slave labor camps, where inmates were worked to death.

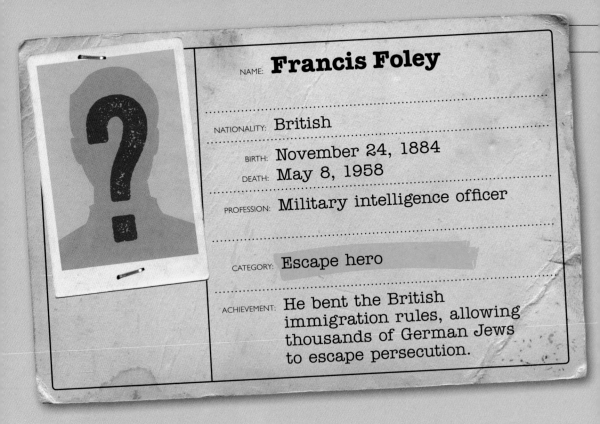

NAME: **Francis Foley**

NATIONALITY: British

BIRTH: November 24, 1884
DEATH: May 8, 1958

PROFESSION: Military intelligence officer

CATEGORY: Escape hero

ACHIEVEMENT: He bent the British immigration rules, allowing thousands of German Jews to escape persecution.

A military intelligence officer stationed at the British Embassy in Berlin, Francis Foley spied on the increasingly belligerent Nazi Germany. At the same time, using his cover as passport and visa officer, he broke the UK's strict immigration rules, allowing over 8,000 Jews to emigrate to Britain and her territories, and Mandatory Palestine.

Twenty-one British men and women are honored at *Yad Vashem* as "Righteous Among the Nations." It is typical of Francis Foley, the unassuming middle-aged man, who stares fixedly at the camera through a pair of round spectacles in his passport photograph, that very few people knew that, between 1935 and 1939, he used his official position at the British Embassy in Berlin to save the lives of over 8,000 German Jews. Full recognition came four decades after his death, when he was made a "Righteous Gentile" in 1999. Since then, memorials to Foley have been unveiled in his native Somerset and in Berlin.

Spymaster
A pupil of the Roman Catholic Stonyhurst College, Foley initially wanted to become a priest. He began his training at a seminary in France but

changed his mind and switched to the study of Classics at the University of Poitiers. After graduating, he spent time traveling around Europe, becoming fluent in French and German.

Foley fought in World War I, was captured, but managed to escape thanks to his language skills. In the summer of 1918, he joined British Military Intelligence and ran spy networks in France, Belgium, and the Netherlands. After the end of the war, he transferred to the body supervising German compliance with the conditions of the Versailles Treaty, where he worked until it was wound up in 1927.

Our man in Berlin

Foley's next job was as passport and visa officer at the British Embassy in Berlin, but at the same time he was working for British Intelligence and running a network of spies that reported to him on German military R&D. During the 1930s, after Hitler had seized control of the German state, Foley's positions as a spy and diplomat gave him a much better understanding of what was happening to German Jews than his superiors in London.

Although the global economic situation was disastrous after the Wall Street Crash of 1929, and there were strict quotas governing immigration to Britain and the territories it controlled, including Mandatory Palestine, Foley bent the rules by issuing visas to thousands of Jewish families so that they could escape persecution in Germany. Although he was not included among the embassy staff who benefited from diplomatic immunity, Foley risked his life and liberty by going to concentration camps to issue Jewish inmates with British passports that ensured their release.

ABOVE:
Memorial statue to Francis Foley in his hometown of Highbridge, in the UK, to honor a man who shunned the limelight.

Once war had been declared, Foley was recalled to London to help organize and supervise the Twenty Committee's Double-Cross network (see Feature, p. 83) of double agents in Germany and occupied Europe. He continued in intelligence work after the war, returning to Berlin as part of the British team sent to track down and arrest German war criminals.

NAME: **Varian Fry**

NATIONALITY: American

BIRTH: October 15, 1907
DEATH: September 13, 1967

PROFESSION: Journalist

CATEGORY: Escape hero

ACHIEVEMENT: He saved thousands of Jewish refugees from arrest and deportation from occupied France.

As a foreign correspondent, Varian Fry witnessed the mistreatment of Jews in prewar Berlin. With very limited support from the U.S. government, he traveled to France, where he set up an escape network, helping prominent academics, artists, and politicians escape to the safety of the USA and neutral countries.

As we saw in the entry on Virginia Hall (pp. 58–61), in the first three years of the war, the USA had very limited overseas intelligence capabilities, compared to the UK, France, and the Soviet Union. Although the USA had J. Edgar Hoover's formidable FBI to ensure its internal security, the lack of a prewar intelligence agency to coordinate all overseas espionage proved extremely costly, leading ultimately to the failure to foresee Japan's attack on Pearl Harbor in 1941. This lack of intelligence preparedness can be explained by a decade of American isolationism, during which time many U.S. politicians turned their backs on the world, adopting a noninterventionist, neutral stance, determined that the country should not be dragged into another European war.

Fortunately for the world, and for the USA itself, many of its citizens refused to abide by American neutrality, and, like Hall, enthusiastically entered the fight against Hitler and the Nazis long before the U.S. government declared war on the Axis powers in 1941. Another American citizen who exploited U.S. neutrality to maximum effect is the subject of this entry, journalist Varian Fry. Without him, the arts, literature, social sciences, and sciences of the postwar world would have been considerably diminished, because they would have lost

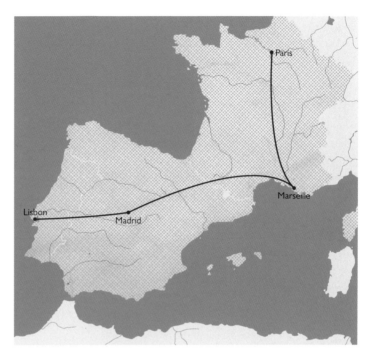

such luminaries as artists Marc Chagall (1887–1985) and Max Ernst (1891–1976), social scientists Hannah Arendt (1906–75) and Claude Lévi-Strauss (1908–2009), and writer Arthur Koestler (1905–83), who were among the 6,150 European refugees that Fry managed to get to the safety of American soil.

From New Jersey to Berlin

Like many other men and women who were destined to play a leading role in the secret war, there is little in Fry's childhood that explains why he risked his life and liberty to help people with whom he had no personal, religious, or national connection. The son of a Protestant family, he was born in New York but grew up in the Garden State, after his stockbroker father moved his family across the Hudson to Ridgewood, New Jersey. During World War I, like many other patriotic American schoolboys, he raised funds for the American Red Cross. He graduated from high school in 1926, and went on to study at Harvard University, where he founded the *Hound & Horn* literary magazine. While at Harvard, Fry's circle included Jewish friends, including writer, impresario, and philanthropist Lincoln Kirstein (1907–96).

After graduation, Fry got a job on *The Living Age*, a long-established literary periodical based in Boston. In 1935, he traveled to Berlin as one of the magazine's overseas correspondents, where he witnessed the persecution of German Jews. It was a decisive moment for Fry, who later wrote about what he had seen: "There are some things so horrible that decent men and women find them impossible to believe, so monstrous that the

civilized world recoils incredulous before them." He declared, "I could not remain idle as long as I had any chances at all of saving even a few of its intended victims." Back in New York, and now an editor for the Foreign Policy Association, Fry wrote books and articles about the situation in Europe, trying to change hearts and minds within the isolationist U.S. administration.

Fry to the rescue

After Hitler seized power in Germany and enacted the Reich's anti-Semitic laws, many prominent Jewish and anti-Nazi academics, artists, scientists, and politicians left the country. The fortunate few, like physicist Albert Einstein, made it to the USA. But many were unable to make it further than neighboring France, Belgium, or the Netherlands. After the fall of France in 1940, these refugees, plus a large group from France itself, were again in imminent danger of arrest and deportation by the *Gestapo* and the *Milice Française*, if they remained in German- or Vichy-controlled territory.

Frustrated by the lack of action on the part of the American government, Fry traveled to Marseilles in Vichy France as the representative of the newly formed Emergency Rescue Committee. He arrived with $3,000 ($50,000 in 2015) and a meager 200 refugee visas granted to him by the U.S. Immigration Department. What Fry soon discovered was that several thousand refugees, including many prominent Jewish and anti-Nazi academics, politicians, writers, and artists needed his help. The numbers coming to his hotel were so great that he was forced to rent a nearby office,

ABOVE:

A member of the SA pictured in front of a Jewish shop in Berlin, 1933. The sign reads: "Germans! Defend yourselves! Do not buy from Jews!"

which was staffed by French sympathizers and two American expatriates, artist Miriam Davenport (1915–99) and heiress Mary Jayne Gold (1909–97).

For 13 months, Fry saw up to 70 refugees a day. Unable to turn anyone away for fear that he might learn later that they had been sent to a concentration camp, Fry arranged for the refugees to be hidden in safe houses before they were smuggled across the Spanish border, and then Portugal, from where they left for the United States. Another route to the USA was by ship, from Marseilles to the French Caribbean island of Martinique. The Vichy government expelled Fry from France in September 1941, by which time he had succeeded in saving an estimated 6,150 people. He is one of the four American citizens honored by *Yad Vashem* as a "Righteous Gentile."

ABOVE:
Senior officials in the French *Gestapo*, photographed outside their Paris HQ. The Nazi secret service was a formidably efficient enemy of the Resistance.

FEATURE **Among the righteous**

We can get an idea of the scale of the secret war's escape operations by the recognition accorded to escape heroes by the Shoah Martyrs' and Heroes' Remembrance Authority, established as part of *Yad Vashem* in 1953. The authority recognized 25,685 men and women (as of January 1, 2015) from 45 countries as "Righteous Gentiles." A commission, headed by a justice of the Supreme Court of Israel, decides on the award, basing itself on the following four criteria: nomination by a Jewish person; help was given to practicing Jews who were not family members; assistance was substantial and repeated, and given without expectation of financial reward other than expenses for food and shelter. The countries whose Jewish communities were most affected by the Holocaust have the majority of recipients: Poland (6,532), the Netherlands (5,413), France (3,853), Ukraine (2,515), Belgium (1,690), Lithuania (877), and Hungary (823).

NAME: **Miep Gies**

NATIONALITY: Austrian and Dutch

BIRTH: February 15, 1909
DEATH: January 11, 2010

PROFESSION: Office worker

CATEGORY: Escape hero

ACHIEVEMENT: She helped the Frank family hide from the *Gestapo* during their two-year concealment.

A refugee in the Netherlands after World War I, Miep Gies was Austrian by birth. She worked for Otto Frank, who had moved his family from Aachen to Amsterdam to escape Nazi persecution. After Germany occupied the Netherlands, Gies helped the Franks during their two years in hiding.

At the time of writing, the European Union is experiencing what is referred to in the media as "the largest refugee crisis since World War II." When compared to the population movements caused by the two world wars, the scale of the Syrian crisis is, in numerical terms at least, relatively minor. For the people involved, of course, their flight from war and persecution is just as difficult and tragic.

World War I led to the dismemberment of four empires: Czarist Russia, Ottoman Turkey, the Second German Reich, and Austro-Hungary. The map of Europe was redrawn, and the creation of new nations triggered large population shifts, as ethnic and cultural minorities were forced to leave countries where they were no longer welcome. Among the new states created by well-meaning committees, the defunct

Czechoslovakia and Yugoslavia created flashpoints that continued to plague Europe until the end of the 20th century.

In the years immediately following their defeat, Germany and Austria were prey to major social, political, and economic upheavals, which sparked revolutions and civil wars and caused mass unemployment and severe food shortages, leading to a second exodus of refugees and economic migrants. Miep Gies was one of this postwar wave of refugees, and her childhood experiences would have given her a deep and abiding understanding of the terrible plight of German Jewish refugees Otto Frank (1889–1980), his wife Edith (1900–45), and his two daughters, Margot (1926–45) and Anne (1929–45).

From Vienna to Amsterdam

Gies was born Hermine Santruschitz in Vienna, when it was still the capital of a vast, multinational empire. She was just nine years old when the world that she knew came to an abrupt end. The last emperor abdicated and the Austro-Hungarian Empire, which could trace its origins back to the 10th-century Holy Roman Empire, ceased to exist. Austria, now reduced to a rump state, could barely feed its people. In 1920, a Dutch working-class couple with six children of their own took in a little Austrian girl, whom they called Miep, the name that she kept for the rest of her life.

Although Gies chose to remain in the Netherlands with her foster family, the German authorities considered her to be German. In 1938, Germany had imposed the *Anschluss*—the forced union of Austria and Germany. In 1940, when the Germans invaded the Netherlands, they ordered Gies to join the local Nazi Party. When she refused, they cancelled her passport and ordered her back to Austria. In order to obtain Dutch citizenship and avoid deportation, she hurriedly married her Dutch fiancé, Jan Gies (1905–93) in July 1941.

ABOVE:
In happier times: Otto and Anne Frank at Miep Gies' wedding in July 1941, before they were forced to go into hiding to avoid deportation.

ABOVE:
A smiling Anne Frank.

Friends in need

After graduating from high school,
Gies got a job with an accountancy
firm and, in 1933, was recruited by
Otto Frank to work for the firm he
had set up in Amsterdam. A native of
Frankfurt, Otto knew that he would
have to leave Germany to save his
family once Hitler had been voted
into power. Just after the Nazi victory
at the polls in March 1933, he moved
his family to Aachen, a town
bordering Belgium and the
Netherlands, where the family stayed
with Edith Frank's mother.

Otto stayed on in Frankfurt, but
when he was offered the job of
establishing a Dutch subsidiary of
German manufacturer of pectin and
spices, Opekta, he accepted, seeing
the opportunity as an ideal means of
getting himself and his family out of
Germany. By the beginning of 1934,
Edith, Anne, and Margot had joined
Otto in Amsterdam. The Franks were
among 300,000 Jews who, between 1933 and 1939, chose exile over the
ever-worsening anti-Semitic persecution that the Nazis unleashed in
Germany. Unfortunately, the Franks did not travel far enough.

Otto attempted and failed to obtain U.S. and Cuban visas for himself
and his family in 1938 and again in 1941. But after the Germans had
occupied the Netherlands in May 1940, the Franks were trapped. He
managed to avoid the confiscation of his firm by transferring ownership
to non-Jewish friends, and was thus able to maintain a small income
to support his family.

Into hiding

On July 6, 1942, to avoid being deported to the death camps, Otto and his family hid in an upper-floor annex of the Opekta business premises on Prinsengracht, now the site of the Anne Frank House Museum. The Franks shared their hiding place with the van Pels family and Fritz Pfeffer (1899–1944). They survived thanks to Otto's colleagues, Johannes Kleiman (1896–1959), Victor Kugler (1900–81), Elisabeth Voskuijl (1919–83), and Gies, who, at great risk to themselves, provided the refugees with the necessities of life. The entrance to the annex was hidden behind a bookcase, and when Gies went shopping for food for the Franks, she had to make sure not to give them away by buying or carrying too much at one time.

The Franks remained hidden for two years, until, in August 1944, they were betrayed by an unidentified informant. The Opekta premises were raided by the SS, and the Franks were deported to Auschwitz-Birkenau. Otto was the only one to survive. Edith died of starvation in Auschwitz; and Anne and Margot both died at Bergen-Belsen concentration camp, possibly in a typhus epidemic that was ravaging the camp in the early months of 1945. Gies managed to evade arrest because her *Gestapo* interrogator was a fellow Viennese.

FEATURE **Twice saved**

One of the most moving firsthand testimonies of the Nazi persecution of European Jews, Anne Frank's *The Diary of a Young Girl* (1952), originally published in Dutch in 1947 as *Het Achterhuis. Dagboekbrieven 14 Juni 1942 – 1 Augustus 1944* (*The Annex: Diary Notes June 14, 1942—August 1, 1944*), was almost destroyed before it could see be published. Had the *Gestapo* found and read Anne's diary, written as a series of letters to her imaginary best friend "Kitty," it would have ended in the trash or the incinerator. Fortunately, the Germans probably did not think anything written by a Jew was worth reading. But Miep Gies, who found the diary and hid it in her desk until the end of the war, said that she, too, would have burned it had she read it, because it listed the names of the people who had helped the Franks during their concealment.

LEFT:
The bookcase that concealed the door into the annex where the Franks and several other Jewish refugees succeeded in hiding for two years.

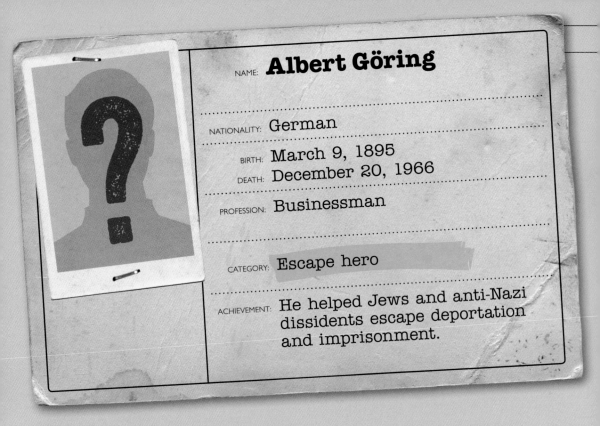

NAME: **Albert Göring**

NATIONALITY: German

BIRTH: March 9, 1895
DEATH: December 20, 1966

PROFESSION: Businessman

CATEGORY: Escape hero

ACHIEVEMENT: He helped Jews and anti-Nazi dissidents escape deportation and imprisonment.

Unlike his older brother, Hermann Göring, head of the *Luftwaffe*, Albert Göring despised the Nazis. He strove to oppose them by every means at his disposal, saving Jews and anti-Nazi dissidents, while at the same time using his relationship with Hermann to ensure immunity from arrest and thus his own survival.

The case of Albert Göring, *Reichsmarschall* Hermann Göring's (1893–1946) younger brother, casts an interesting light on the upper echelons of German society and their relationship with the Nazi Party. Although many plotters in the Black Orchestra came from aristocratic, military backgrounds, just as many in the Prussian Junker class enthusiastically embraced Nazism. But the contrasting attitudes of the Göring brothers suggests that pro- or anti-Nazi sympathies were not always decided by class; some were determined by experience and personal circumstances.

Sibling rivalry
The Göring brothers benefited from a privileged upbringing, growing up in a castle owned by their godfather, Hermann von Epenstein. But even

here, things were not quite what they seemed, because von Epenstein was Jewish by descent and hence a Nazi target. One explanation as to why the elder was an early Nazi adherent, while the other was just as steadfast in his opposition, is that Albert was the illegitimate son of von Epenstein, making him part Jewish. This theory is improbable, not least because Albert's parents were living overseas, away from Epenstein, when he was conceived.

A simpler explanation, credible to anyone who has grown up with an older brother and sister, is of sibling rivalry, pitching the more successful, overbearing Hermann, World War I ace and Nazi *Reichsmarschall*, against the foppish Albert, who was not expected to amount to much, and who may have resented living in his older brother's rather expansive shadow.

Suspending disbelief

After the war, few believed that Albert had not taken part in his brother's many crimes. The brothers were imprisoned together and appeared as defendants at the Nuremberg Trials (1946–47). But two investigations into Albert's character and wartime activities not only exonerated him but proved that he had taken an active part in the German resistance against the Nazis. Using his privileged position and, when he needed to, his brother's name and good offices, he got an unconfirmed number of Jews and anti-Nazi dissidents freed from prison and helped them to escape to neutral countries.

ABOVE:
Albert's brother Hermann was a close associate of Hitler during his rise to power and a leading figure in the Nazi regime until the end of the war.

After he was appointed an executive at a Czechoslovak arms manufacturer, Skoda Works, he established links with the Czech resistance and facilitated sabotage of the firm's plants. On several occasions he sent trucks to concentration camps to requisition slave laborers for the firm, but once the trucks were in open country, he ordered that the detainees to be released. Although many of those he saved testified on his behalf and even helped him after the war, when he lived in straitened circumstances, Albert never received recognition for his resistance activities. The recent publication of a biography of Albert Göring prompted *The Jewish Chronicle* to call for his recognition by *Yad Vashem* as a "Righteous Gentile."

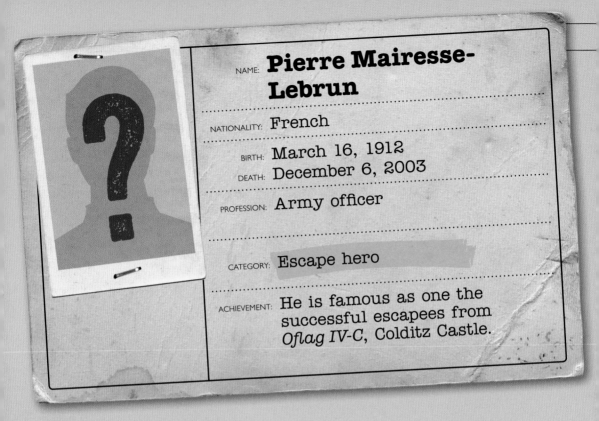

NAME: **Pierre Mairesse-Lebrun**

NATIONALITY: French

BIRTH: March 16, 1912

DEATH: December 6, 2003

PROFESSION: Army officer

CATEGORY: Escape hero

ACHIEVEMENT: He is famous as one the successful escapees from *Oflag IV-C*, Colditz Castle.

A French army officer who earned his place at Colditz Castle early in World War II, Pierre Mairesse-Lebrun is notable among the inmates of *Oflag IV-C* in that he succeeded in escaping at his second attempt, evaded recapture by the Germans, and returned to the fight.

This section opened with the exploits of Douglas Bader (pp. 176–179), who never let his disability get in the way of what he saw as his POW's duty to "goon bait"—that is, to make his German captors' lives as difficult as possible. Once in Colditz, Bader was held back from any further escape attempts by his artificial limbs and his fame, both of which made him easily identifiable and thus a hindrance to fellow escapees.

Escaping from Colditz Castle would have challenged a much fitter person, but in the summer of 1941, the man who accepted that challenge with alacrity on two occasions was French cavalry officer Pierre Mairesse-Lebrun. His escape was not without difficulty. While traveling through a mountainous region of Spain on his way to French North Africa, he injured his spine, temporarily paralyzing his legs.

Testing the water

The inmates of Colditz had petitioned the commandant to be allowed to exercise in the estate's park, which was conveniently located below the castle, and was protected by an inner barbed-wire fence and an outer wall that was 10–16 feet (3–5m) high. For his first escape attempt, in June 1941, Mairesse-Lebrun arranged for a much smaller inmate to be smuggled into the park under the clothes of another officer during the exercise period. The Frenchman hid in the roof space of a small pavilion in the park, and when it was time to return to the castle, the other inmate was there to take Mairesse-Lebrun's place, ensuring that the subsequent headcount would present the same number of inmates returning from the park as had initially left. After successfully evading the guard dogs sent into the park to smell out any would-be escapees, Mairesse-Lebrun made it as far as a railway station 5 miles (8km) away, but was arrested when trying to buy his ticket with a prewar banknote.

BELOW:
Mairesse-Lebrun's epic journey after his escape from Colditz. Starting out on foot, he completed the 400-mile (640km) journey on a stolen bicycle.

Second time's a charm

Mairesse-Lebrun's second attempt, in July 1941, was far more daring in its simplicity. Having trained for several weeks with runs and exercise sessions, he positioned an accomplice in front of the inner fence. At a given signal, Mairesse-Lebrun ran full speed toward him. As the disbelieving German guards looked on, Mairesse-Lebrun's comrade made a stirrup with his hands and heaved the Frenchman over the fence. He zigzagged his way to the outer wall, drawing the guards' fire, which gave him time to get over the wall when they reloaded. Evading capture by traveling at night, he walked to the Saxon town of Zwickau, 43 miles (70km) south of Colditz, where he stole a bicycle. Posing as a touring cyclist, he succeeded in reaching the safety of neutral Switzerland after a ride of some 400 miles (640km).

BELGIUM

GERMANY

FRANCE

Colditz Castle
Zwickau
Nuremberg
Stuttgart
Zurich
SWITZERLAND

—— On foot
········ By bicycle

NAME: **Hugh O'Flaherty**

NATIONALITY: Irish

BIRTH: February 28, 1898
DEATH: October 30, 1963

PROFESSION: Catholic priest

CATEGORY: Escape hero

ACHIEVEMENT: After the German occupation of Rome, he saved the lives of of thousands of Allied POWs and Jews.

Nicknamed the Vatican's "Scarlet Pimpernel," Hugh O'Flaherty used his status as a citizen of the neutral Republic of Ireland, allied to the inviolability of the sovereign soil of Vatican City, to save the lives of Italian Jews, anti-Nazi dissidents, and Allied POWs released after Mussolini had been deposed.

After the war, the Catholic Church received a very mixed press about whether it had done enough to denounce and oppose the Holocaust. The Vatican's sternest critics accused it of a culpable silence that was tantamount to complicity with the Nazis, while others cited the examples of senior Church figures, two of whom are featured in this book: Bishop Clemens von Galen (pp. 144–147), who denounced Nazi ideology from the pulpit, and the subject of this entry, Monsignor Hugh O'Flaherty, who hid Jews and Allied POWs in the Vatican.

It is the case that the papal encyclical *Mit brennender Sorge* of 1937 (see p. 147) and von Clemens' three sermons of 1941 limited themselves to denouncing only the persecution of Catholic Christians of Jewish descent, whom the Germans still considered to be "racially" Jewish, and the T4 forced euthanasia program, and did not specifically condemn the persecution of practicing Jews. However, they were written before the Wannsee Conference had initiated the full implementation of the Final Solution on January 20, 1942. Without offering an apologia for the actions of the wartime Roman Catholic Church and the papacies of Pius XI and XII, it is important to note that the church's attitudes and behavior were mirrored by those of many governments, which adopted a kind of willful denial about the Holocaust until the liberation of the death camps in 1945.

Although Mussolini's fascist regime was Hitler's oldest and closest ally, it had been somewhat less fervant than the Nazis when adopting the Reich's draconian anti-Jewish race laws. But after Mussolini had been deposed in July 1943 and the new government had declared war on its former ally, the Germans invaded Italy, bringing with them the full armory of anti-Semitic measures they had imposed across the rest of occupied Europe. Although they garrisoned Rome, the Germans did not dare violate papal neutrality by occupying Vatican City, which immediately became a focus for the Italian resistance and a safe-haven for Jews, anti-Nazi dissidents, and the Allied POWs who had been released after Mussolini's fall from power but were at risk of rearrest by the SS.

ABOVE:
As a high-ranking official of the Roman Curia, O'Flaherty could count on the loyalty of faithful Catholics in both the Allied and Axis camps.

Enemy turned ally

Hugh O'Flaherty was a seminarian in Ireland during the Irish War of Independence (1919–21), which led to the establishment of an independent Irish Free State. Like many of his countrymen, he had no love for his former British masters, and his motivation for helping many of the British POWs stranded in Italy was not some residual or misplaced loyalty to the Crown but what he saw as a humanitarian duty to his fellow man. After the war, that same duty of care led him to befriend Herbert Kappler (1907–78), SD and *Gestapo* chief in Rome, who had sworn to have him executed and who had been sentenced to life imprisonment for war crimes.

Having completed his training in Rome, O'Flaherty was ordained in 1925. After obtaining his doctorate in theology, he served in the Sacred Congregation for the Propagation of the Faith, as well as in the Vatican diplomatic service, before being appointed to the senior post of notary of the Holy Office.

Hide and seek

From September 1943, the situation in Rome became much more dangerous for the enemies of the Nazis. The Allies had landed in southern Italy and were gradually pushing their way northward. Approximately 75,000 Allied POWs, who had been released, were forced to go into hiding. About 4,000, around half of whom were British, made their way to the Vatican, where they sought out the English-speaking Irish Embassy to the Holy See and Monsignor O'Flaherty, who had made pastoral visits to POW camps during the first four years of the war.

BELOW:
The Church of St. Thomas of Villanova in Castel Gandolfo, one of the many Vatican buildings in which O'Flaherty hid Jews, political dissidents, and Allied POWs.

Until June 4, 1944, when the Americans marched unopposed into Rome, the SS, O'Flaherty, and some 6,500 Allied POWS, Jews, and anti-German dissidents played a gigantic game of Roman hide and seek. O'Flaherty arranged for the refugees to be hidden in the Vatican itself and in the papal fortress of Castel Gandolfo, where they posed as members of the Palatine Guard, and in convents, monasteries, religious colleges, churches, and private homes all over the city. The operation was financed from Church funds and donations by members of the Roman aristocracy.

A narrow escape

Once the Germans realized that their nemesis was a priest and identified O'Flaherty, they made repeated attempts to arrest or assassinate him. Kappler had a line painted on the edge of St. Peter's Square, warning O'Flaherty through the German ambassador to the Holy See that, if he

FEATURE | **Blessed are the peacemakers**

One possible reason Hitler wanted Pius XII kidnapped or killed in 1943 (see Feature, p. 139) was that he had discovered the Pope's role in the Black Orchestra resistance network (see Feature, p. 170) and held him complicit in their repeated attempts to assassinate him. In the first winter of the war, Josef Müller (1898–1979), a lawyer and *Abwehr* agent, who was also a devout Catholic, contacted the Pope's secretary, Robert Leiber (1887–1967), to establish communications between resistance leaders Hans von Dohnányi (1902–45), Ludwig Beck (pp. 120–123), and Wilhelm Canaris (pp. 136–139), and the British foreign secretary, Lord Halifax (1881–1959). During several secret trips to Rome, Müller carried documents that listed the composition of the civilian government that would follow a successful military coup against Hitler. Leiber gave the documents to the Pope, who passed them on to Sir D'Arcy Osborne (1884–1964), British minister to the Vatican, who forwarded them to London.

crossed it, he would be shot on sight. On one occasion, when O'Flaherty was visiting a prominent Roman aristocrat and staunch anti-Nazi, Prince Filippo Doria Pamphili, the SS cornered him in the prince's palace. Hiding in the cellars, he saw that a coal delivery was in progress. Stripping off his clerical garb and covering himself in coal dust, O'Flaherty escaped with the help of the delivery men, who passed him off as one of their own. They dropped him off at a nearby church, where he cleaned himself up before calmly walking back to the Vatican.

ABOVE:

Pius XII was accused of complicity with the Germans, but with O'Flaherty, the Church could claim they had done what they could for Italian Jews.

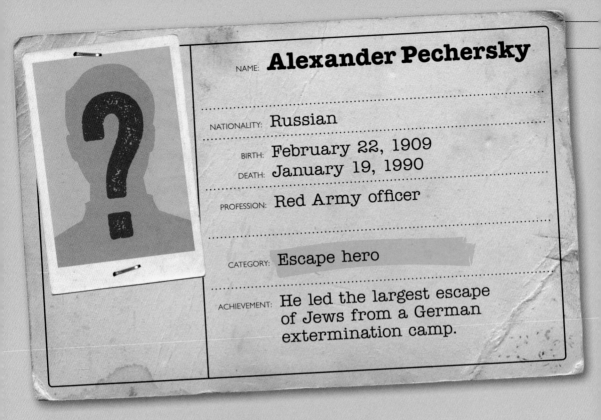

NAME: **Alexander Pechersky**

NATIONALITY: Russian

BIRTH: February 22, 1909

DEATH: January 19, 1990

PROFESSION: Red Army officer

CATEGORY: Escape hero

ACHIEVEMENT: He led the largest escape of Jews from a German extermination camp.

As an officer in the Soviet Red Army, Alexander Pechersky was first interned with other Russian POWs, but when he was identified as Jewish, he was sent to Sobibór labor and extermination camp. Not content to escape on his own, he organized a mass revolt and breakout from the camp.

When reading accounts of the Holocaust, and in particular of the fate of the estimated 3.5 million Jews who lost their lives in the death camps of Auschwitz-Birkenau (an estimated 1,100,000 murdered), Treblinka (870,000), Belzec (600,000), Madjanek (360,000), Chelmno (320,000), and Sobibór (250,000), we are haunted by images of long lines of men, women, and children, wrapped up against the cold, tightly clasping suitcases, bundles, and bags, in the expectation that life, no matter how hard, would continue. We know of course that many would meet their deaths within a few hours of such photos being taken.

Perhaps the oldest among them, who remembered the eastern European and Russian pogroms, might have feared the worst, but how

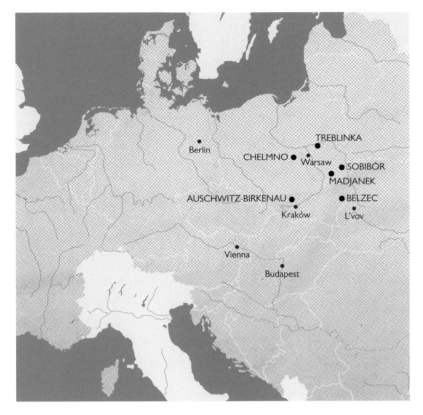

could those arriving from civilized, cosmopolitan Paris, Amsterdam, Brussels, Warsaw and Prague ever have imagined what lay in wait? The inhumanity of the camps must have been beyond the comprehension of many of them—the hell of forced labor, disease, starvation, and mass murder, imposed by people apparently devoid of human feeling.

In a chilling piece of testimony at his trial, the commandant of Auschwitz-Birkenau explained the differences between the older and newer extermination camps:

> *Another improvement we made was that we built the gas chambers to*
> *accommodate 2,000 people at one time ... Still another improvement*
> *was that at Treblinka the victims almost always knew that they were*
> *to be exterminated and at Auschwitz we managed to fool them into*
> *thinking that they were going to be deloused.*

Two earlier entries, featuring Mordechai Anielewicz (pp. 116–119) and Ariadna Scriabina (pp. 164–167), expose the lie that most Jews accepted their fate with shocked bemusement or fatalistic resignation. There were acts of heroic resistance both inside and outside the death camps, but one of the most extraordinary was the revolt and mass escape from Sobibór that forced SS chief Heinrich Himmler to close the camp and have the site cleared and planted with trees so that the victory of the "lesser races" over their "Aryan masters" was forever obliterated.

From POW to slave laborer

A native of the Czarist Poltava Governorate (now Ukraine), Red Army lieutenant Alexander Pechersky was extremely lucky to have survived the war at all. After he was captured by the *Wehrmacht* on the outskirts of Moscow in the fall of 1941, he contracted typhus, recovering after a 7-month illness. As a captured Soviet officer, however, he could have been summarily executed at any time, but the risk worsened considerably when a routine medical forced him to admit that he was a Jew. He was moved from a POW to a labor camp, where, in Pechersky's words, "The German Nazi camp commandant didn't let a single day pass without killing someone."

Even after his escape from the Sobibór death camp, Pechersky's troubles were far from over. Dictator Joseph Stalin (1878–1953) had decreed that all Red Army soldiers who had surrendered to the Germans were traitors to the Soviet Union, assigning them to penal regiments that fought the toughest engagements until the end of the

war. Postwar, Pechersky, like Leopold Trepper (pp. 102–105), was arrested and imprisoned during an anti-Jewish pogrom. He was not released until after the dictator's death, but even then the official persecution did not stop. Although he was called upon to testify at various international trials related to Sobibór, the KGB forbade him to leave the country.

The great escape

On September 23, 1943, Pechersky arrived at Sobibór extermination camp in a group of over 2,000 civilian Jews and Soviet Jewish POWs. A few hours later, only 80 prisoners, including Pechersky, remained alive, destined to be used as slave laborers. He quickly learned the fate of the trainloads of Jewish civilians that arrived daily from Russia, France, Poland, Germany, the Netherlands, and Czechoslovakia. He decided there and then that he would escape, but also vowed that he would not abandon the other inmates of the camp to be tortured and murdered by the Germans.

Pechersky's escape plan was ready three weeks later. On November 14, the inmates lured SS and Ukrainian guards into the camp's workshops where they killed them with homemade axes and knives and tools recovered from the corpses of gassed Jews. Armed with the weapons taken from the dead guards, the escapees obtained more from the garrison's barracks. When the camp commandant discovered that his second in command had been killed, the fighting began in earnest. Perchesky led the rebels into the nearby forest. Of the 550 Jewish inmates, 420

FEATURE # Himmler's death squads

The secret war has many dark episodes, but none darker than the Third Reich's extermination policies. Of the estimated 5.5–6.5 million Jews who lost their lives between 1938 and 1945, over half died in six Polish death camps, but another 1–1.3 million Jews were murdered in cold blood by *Einsatzgruppen* (task forces), paramilitary killing squads of the SS, which were sent into occupied eastern Europe and Russia between 1941 and 1945. The first *Einsatzgruppen* were formed in 1938 and tasked with implementing the Action T4 forced euthanasia program in Germany, Austria, and the occupied Sudetenland. The crimes of the *Einsatzgruppen* were worst during the invasion of the Soviet Union, when, in addition to Jews, Communist intellectuals and officials, political commissars, and members of Soviet military intelligence were singled out for immediate elimination as a forerunner for the extermination of all Slavs whose lands were intended for "Aryan" colonists.

took part in the uprising; 80 were killed during the escape; and 170 were recaptured in the subsequent search and immediately executed, along with those who had remained in the camp. But 53 Polish Jewish escapees survived the war and lived to testify at the trials of their guards.

About 50 prisoners stayed with Pechersky, but he explained after the war that he had already decided that their chances of survival were much greater if they split up. He slipped away from the group and later joined Jewish partisans who were hiding out in the forest. He remained with them until Poland was liberated by the Red Army.

ABOVE:

Heinrich Himmler visiting one of the many concentration, forced labor, and extermination camps run by the SS in occupied Europe.

NAME:	**Oskar Schindler**
NATIONALITY:	Czechoslovak and German
BIRTH:	April 28, 1908
DEATH:	October 9, 1974
PROFESSION:	Industrialist
CATEGORY:	Escape hero
ACHIEVEMENT:	He risked his life to save Jewish workers in his factory from deportation to concentration camps.

A hard-drinking, high-living, war-profiteering playboy, Oscar Schindler was a highly unlikely man to become a Holocaust hero. He spent the money he made through black market speculation and the kitchenware factory he somewhat dubiously acquired in German-occupied Kraków to save 1,098 Jews from certain death in the gas chambers.

On the face of it, German businessman Oskar Schindler was a likeable but selfish rogue, who was solely out for himself and single-minded when it came making the money needed to live the high life. He spied for the *Abwehr* in his native Sudetenland, when it was part of Czechoslovakia, and was arrested by the Czechs for espionage and sentenced to two years in prison. When the Germans finally marched into Czechoslovakia in March 1939, Schindler was one of the pro-Nazi political prisoners they set free.

Following Germany's invasion of Poland in September 1939, it was natural for Schindler to follow the invading armies to Kraków—a Polish city he knew well from peacetime visits. He was confident that he would easily find ways of profiting from the continuing conflict by fair means or foul. His first move was to buy a bankrupt kitchenware factory from its Jewish owners and to reopen it in January 1940. A potent blend of charm, personality, and a fair amount of bribery helped him to secure lucrative army and SS contracts for his pots and pans, assuring his business' financial success.

Schindler's lists

One of the first people Schindler hired to help him run his new business was Itzhak Stern (1901–69), a Jewish accountant who became his bookkeeper, and who is credited with typing the first of Schindler's several lists of Jews rescued from the Holocaust. It was Stern who advised Schindler to turn to Kraków's Jews to staff the plant. He assured Schindler that they would be a good source of cheap, reliable labor. During the first year of production, the labor force expanded to 300, including 150 Jews. By the end of 1942, he employed 800 men and women.

ABOVE:
Following the invading German army, Schindler went to occupied Poland in search of business opportunities. In Kraków he bought a confiscated homewares factory.

The Jewish workers, now numbering 370, all came from the ghetto the Germans had created in the city. There was no shortage of recruits. "It became a tremendous advantage," Stern recalled several years later, "to be able to leave the ghetto in the daytime and work in a German factory." Although they did not understand why, they realized that, for some reason, Schindler was protecting them. This became obvious when, in June 1942, 14 of Schindler's Jewish workers, including his office manager, Abraham Bankier, were rounded up by the SS as part of a series of random street arrests and forcibly marched off to the train station at Prokocim for immediate deportation. Luckily for them, Edith Kener, who also worked for Schindler, had witnessed the arrest and tracked down Schindler in one of his hangouts to beg him to help them.

ABOVE:
When the Germans began the deportation of Jews from the Kraków Ghetto to the extermination camps, Schindler risked his life to protect his Jewish workers.

Schindler acted immediately. He raced to the station and marched up and down the platform, where the freight cars of the deportation train had been standing waiting all day, calling out Bankier's name. When he finally heard a muffled response, he demanded the prisoners' immediate release, telling the SS officer in charge of the transport that they were essential workers and their continued detention would sabotage the war effort. He dropped the names of some of his high-ranking Nazi friends into the conversation to reinforce his point. Eventually, after securing the prisoners' release, he personally escorted them back to his factory and safety.

Increasing scrutiny

As implementation of the Final Solution progressed, Schindler's own position started to become insecure. First, he was ordered to switch production in his factory from enamelware to the manufacture of shell cases. If he refused, he was told, the factory would be shut down. Then he was actually arrested by the *Gestapo* as part of its ongoing investigation into alleged black market dealings. The company's books were seized and examined for irregularities. However, pressure from above brought about Schindler's release within a few hours.

Schindler found himself dealing more and more with the SS. In early 1943, the Nazis ordered the Kraków Ghetto to be liquidated. Jews fit enough to work were to be transported to labor camps. Those who were not were to be exterminated on the spot or sent to the gas chambers. Amon Goeth (1908–46), the young SS officer in charge of the Płaszów labor camp just outside the city, was put in command of the operation. Goeth was a ruthless sadist who took pleasure in his work. Rena Finder, then a 14-year-old girl, who managed to survive the war to testify at Goeth's trial for war crimes, said he

FEATURE **Why Schindler?**

Just what motivated Schindler to act as he did, risking his own life, is still something of a mystery. His wife, Emilia, offered her own explanation in the memoirs she published after the couple had become estranged. "In spite of his flaws," she wrote, "Oskar had a big heart and was always ready to help whoever was in need." He was affable, kind, extremely generous, and charitable, but, at the same time, not mature at all. Schindler himself put it more succinctly in a 1964

interview: "I felt that the Jews were being destroyed," he said. "I had to help them. There was no choice." Whether Schindler actually bribed Amon Goeth, the young SS officer in charge of the Płaszów labor camp, or not is uncertain, but it is probable that he did. In September 1944, Goeth was relieved of his command, arrested by the SS itself, and charged with black market trading.

was "the most vicious and sadistic man" she had ever encountered. Poldek Pfefferberg, another survivor, said simply: "When you saw Goeth, you saw death."

Schindler met Goeth for the first time at a dinner party the camp commandant and his mistress threw to celebrate the completion of his newly constructed villa. He quickly realized the kind of man with whom he would have to deal. To keep his workers out of SS hands, he convinced Goeth that, "in the interests of efficiency," he should be allowed to build a barracks to house them all on a plot of land adjacent to the factory, thus ensuring their survival.

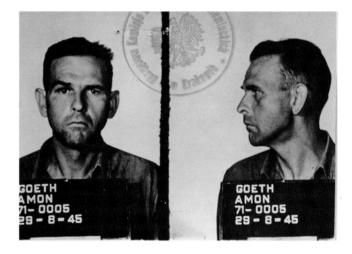

ABOVE:
Mugshot of Amon Goeth, the commandant of the Płaszów labor camp, whom Schindler probably had to bribe to save his Jewish workers.

NAME: **Irena Sendler**

NATIONALITY: Polish

BIRTH: February 15, 1910
DEATH: May 12, 2008

PROFESSION: Social worker

CATEGORY: Escape hero

ACHIEVEMENT: She smuggled thousands of Jewish children out of the Warsaw Ghetto, saving them from death.

A social worker in the municipality of Warsaw, Irena Sendler had opposed anti-Semitism in her native Poland since her student days. During the German occupation, she helped Jewish children escape from the Warsaw Ghetto. Although arrested and tortured, she survived the war, only to face persecution again from the Communist authorities.

Until the mid-18th century, the Polish-Lithuanian Commonwealth was the leading power in eastern Europe, but as the Commonwealth succumbed to internal dissension and external interference, Poland found itself caught between three powerful neighbors: Russia, Austro-Hungary, and Prussia (the Second German Reich from 1871). The result was the repeated partition of Poland between the three expansionist empires that had competing claims over the control of central and eastern Europe. Poland knew two decades as an independent nation from 1918 until 1939, when it was again the victim of a secret treaty between Stalinist Russia and Nazi Germany.

The only way Poland could have ensured its survival in 1939 would have been to ally itself with either the Nazi Reich or the Soviet Union and use one to ward off the other. But to the conservative, Catholic Poles, an alliance with the Communists was anathema, and one with the Nazis was impossible because Hitler regarded the Poles as one of the "inferior races" to be enslaved by the "Aryans" and ultimately eliminated as he expanded Germany's *Lebensraum* (living space) eastward.

Late recognition

At even greater risk was Poland's large Jewish community, which from 1942 was scheduled for total extermination in the six death camps built in occupied Polish territory. It is not surprising that in these circumstances, the country that has the highest number of "Righteous Among the Nations" is Poland, with 6,532 awards, including the subject of this entry, Irena Sendler. Although *Yad Vashem* credits her with 153 Jewish lives saved, the actual number is much higher—up to 2,500. The discrepancy can be explained by the strict criteria on confirmed rescue cases set by *Yad Vashem* and not by a dispute over Sendler's role in helping save thousands of Jewish lives, many of them children orphaned by the Holocaust.

ABOVE:
The Germans built ghettos in the main Polish cities and sealed them from non-Jewish areas. The Warsaw Ghetto was home to around 350,000 Jews.

Although Sendler was honored by *Yad Vashem* in 1965, she was not allowed to go to Israel to receive the award until 1983. Like many other Poles who had resisted the German occupation but remained loyal to Poland's government-in-exile in London, and the *Armia Krajowa* (AK; Home Army) it sponsored, she was suspect in the eyes of the postwar Polish Communist regime. She was temporarily imprisoned and denied any honors for her wartime activities. Her achievements were finally recognized in Poland after the fall of Communism in 1989, and she subsequently received many other awards, but her favorite was the Order of the Smile, given by children to adults who have demonstrated great care and love for children.

ABOVE:
Once the Germans had implemented the Final Solution, they began to empty the Polish ghettos, deporting Polish Jews to the extermination camps.

Like father, like daughter

For several of the secret heroes of World War II featured in this book, it is difficult to understand exactly what motivated them to risk their lives to save others unrelated to themselves. Oskar Schindler (see previous entry) is perhaps a case in point here, as he could have lived out the war like many others did, profiteering and keeping his head down. But with Irena Sendler, we can perhaps find the explanation in her family life.

Irena was the daughter of Stanisław Krzyżanowski (1865–1917), a Polish doctor and a committed Polish Socialist. Although a Christian, he worked mainly among Poland's impoverished Jewish community. He died while treating victims of a typhus epidemic when Irena was just seven years old. No doubt inspired by her father's example, Irena trained as a nurse. When asked many years later why she had risked her life to save Jewish children, she replied, "Every child saved with my help is the justification of my existence on this Earth."

Child smuggler

When the German tanks rolled into Warsaw, Irena was 29 years old and was working as a social worker for the municipality's Welfare Department. In April 1940, the Germans herded the Jewish population of the city and its suburbs into a small area set aside as the Jewish ghetto, giving it an estimated population of between 350,000 and 400,000 inhabitants. In November, the ghetto was sealed off from the surrounding city, and the overcrowding and unsanitary conditions soon caused outbreaks of disease.

Sendler used her position in the Welfare Department to obtain a special pass from the German military authorities to enter the ghetto with the excuse of inspecting its sanitary conditions. The Germans were worried that any outbreak of disease, in particular, epidemic typhus, would rapidly spread from the ghetto and affect the non-Jewish population of the city and its German garrison. Once inside the ghetto, she established links with Jewish resistance and welfare organizations, and began smuggling Jews out, including infants, who were sometimes carried out in packages and suitcases, and then entrusted to the care of non-Jewish families.

In the fall of 1942, after the deportation of two-thirds of the ghetto's population to the Treblinka death camp, Żegota (see Feature, below) was established to help those who had survived. In September 1943, several months after the complete destruction of the ghetto, Żegota appointed Sendler the person in charge of the care of Jewish children. Using the codename "Jolanta," she used her contacts as a social worker to place Jewish children with non-Jewish Polish families and in Catholic convents and orphanages.

FEATURE | **Saving Poland's Jews**

Before World War II, Poland had a Jewish population of 3.5 million Jews; after liberation, it is estimated that 10 percent of that number—just 350,000—had survived the war. Within Poland itself, several organizations collaborated to ensure the survival of Jews in hiding, and to help as many as possible escape the several ghettos that the Germans had established in the country's major cities. Foremost among these was *Rada Pomocy Zydom* (the Polish Council to Aid Jews; also known as the Konrad Zegota Committee or Zegota for short), which operated from December 1942 until the liberation of Poland by the Soviet Union in January 1945. It is estimated that Zegota provided some level of assistance to half of the 100,000 Jews who survived the war by hiding in Poland.

NAME: **Chiune Sugihara**

NATIONALITY: Japanese

BIRTH: January 1, 1900

DEATH: July 31, 1986

PROFESSION: Diplomat

CATEGORY: Escape hero

ACHIEVEMENT: He saved thousands of Polish and Lithuanian Jews by issuing transit visas, enabling them to travel to Japan.

A career diplomat in imperial Japan's Foreign Service, Chiune Sugihara was vice-consul in Kaunas, Lithuania, at the outbreak of the European war. Over a period of two months, he issued thousand of visas to Polish and Lithuanian Jews, which allowed them to travel across the Soviet Union to China and Japan.

Hotsumi Ozaki (pp. 156–157) was the only Japanese to have been executed for high treason during World War II. The near-total absence of internal resistance in Japan indicates a culture that prized loyalty to the emperor, who was held up as the incarnation of the state, above all other civic virtues—sometimes leading to the most absurd acts of self-sacrifice, such as the mass suicide of civilians during the U.S. invasion of Okinawa and the *kamikaze* attacks on Allied warships by young Japanese pilots. But there was another side to imperial Japan that was quite at odds to suicidal devotion to duty—a bureaucratic paralysis born of a terror of confrontation.

Rebel, rebel

The case of Chiune Sugihara, Japanese vice-consul in Kaunas, the prewar capital of Lithuania, illuminates the differences between wartime Germany and Japan. In Germany, the Nazis infiltrated the government so thoroughly that it would have been impossible for a public official to disobey his superiors openly and to actively work against government policy, and, more importantly, get away with it. But when Sugihara issued thousands of Japanese transit visas to refugees, flouting Foreign Ministry rules, he was not arrested, sacked, or even disciplined.

The roots of Sugihara's rebelliousness might be found in his youth. As a student, he deliberately went against his father's wishes and flunked the entrance exam to medical school and chose to study English instead. After graduation, he joined the foreign service, but he remained something of a rebel. In 1935, he resigned from his post in Japanese-occupied Manchuria as a protest against the ill-treatment of Chinese civilians.

Righteous man

Sugihara was in Kaunas when Germany invaded western Poland and Russia occupied eastern Poland and the Baltic States. Polish Jews poured into Lithuania, looking to escape from the Germans, and their numbers were swollen by Lithuanian Jews seeking to escape the Soviets. With most Western diplomatic missions closed, the refugees besieged the Japanese Consulate. Bemused by events but realizing that he must do something, Sugihara repeatedly asked for guidance from Tokyo. On three occasions, the Foreign Ministry merely reiterated its rules: Only travelers with sufficient funds and an onward exit visa from Japan should be issued with a Japanese transit visa.

ABOVE:
One of the thousands of visas that Sugihara issued to Jewish refugees to enable them to transit through Japan to the Dutch colony of Curaçao.

Although many refugees did not meet these criteria, Sugihara issued them with visas. He negotiated with the Soviet authorities to allow the refugees to travel to China and Japan via the Trans-Siberian Express. According to *Yad Vashem*, Sugihara, the only Japanese "Righteous Among the Nations," saved 2,861 Jewish lives, but other sources claim that, because many of the visas were good for entire families, he might have saved as many as 10,000.

NAME: **Raoul Wallenberg**

NATIONALITY: Swedish

BIRTH: August 4, 1912
DEATH: July 17, 1947 (presumed)

PROFESSION: Diplomat

CATEGORY: Escape hero

ACHIEVEMENT: He saved thousands of Jewish lives by issuing them with Swedish passports.

A citizen of neutral Sweden, Raoul Wallenberg was able to travel freely in occupied Europe. In 1944 he was recruited by the U.S. War Refugee Board to rescue Hungarian Jews, who were being systematically exterminated by the Germans. He disappeared mysteriously after the war, arrested by the Soviet authorities, who believed he was an American spy.

Hungary and Sweden adopted very different positions at the outbreak of World War II. Unlike its Scandinavian neighbors, Denmark and Norway, which were occupied by Germany, and Finland, which faced a Soviet invasion in 1940, Sweden maintained its neutrality but at the cost of collaborating with the Third Reich. In her own defense, Sweden cited the example of men like Raoul Wallenberg as evidence that she did all she could to help the victims of the Holocaust, claiming that a neutral Sweden was better than another conquered province of an anti-Semitic German Reich.

Hungary also attempted to retain her independence but chose to do so by joining the Axis alliance and participating in the German invasion of the Soviet Union in 1941. The near wipeout of the Hungarian army during the closing months of the siege of Stalingrad (August 1942–February 1943), forced the resignation of Hungary's regent, Miklós Horthy (1868–1957), and triggered a German invasion of the country in March 1944 to prevent the new government from joining the Allied camp.

SS colonel Adolf Eichmann (1906–62) began the deportation and extermination of the 846,000 Hungarian citizens considered to be Jewish by the Reich's racial laws. By early summer 1944, news of the mass deportations to Auschwitz-Birkenau had reached the Allies. The British prime minister, Winston Churchill, was unequivocal in his condemnation, writing, "The persecution of Jews in Hungary and their expulsion from enemy territory is probably the greatest and most horrible crime ever committed in the whole history of the world." Of course, after the end of the war, the Allies discovered that it was just one of the many heinous crimes that the Nazis had committed.

ABOVE:
Hungary's regent Miklós Horthy allied himself with Hitler, but was deposed when the Hungarian army was destroyed during the Siege of Stalingrad.

Proud of his Jewish descent

Wallenberg was from a prominent Swedish family of diplomats, military men, and businessmen, who was also one-sixteenth Jewish, a part of his heritage of which he was extremely proud. In Europe between the wars, he might have been expected to have a quite different attitude, but in 1930, he had told a friend: "A person like me, who is both a Wallenberg and half-Jewish, can never be defeated." Rather than hiding his Jewish ancestry, he exaggerated it.

After graduating from high school, Wallenberg lived in France for a year and then studied for a degree in architecture at the University of Michigan. He spent his summer vacations hitchhiking across the U.S., which he much preferred to the style of travel that his wealth would have allowed him, saying, "Hitchhiking gives you training in diplomacy and tact." On his return to Sweden in 1936, he started working for the Jewish-owned Central European Trading Company.

ABOVE:
After Horthy fell from power, the Germans invaded Hungary to prevent it from switching sides and joining the Allies.

The president's man

Once the Germans had successfully occupied Hungary, they began the deportation and mass murder of its 846,000-strong Jewish community. At its height the Holocaust in Hungary saw the daily deportation of 12,000 Jews from Hungary's ghettos. By June 1944, an estimated 435,000 Jews had been sent to their deaths in the Auschwitz-Birkenau gas chambers. The scale of the operation could not be kept secret from the Allies, who decided to try to prevent the total destruction of Hungary's Jewish community.

President Franklin D. Roosevelt (1882–1945) instructed the War Refugee Board (WRB) to find a way of rescuing the Hungarian Jews. He sent OSS accountant Iver C. Olsen (1904–60) to Sweden to find someone who could be sent to Budapest, with diplomatic accreditation from the Swedish Ministry of Foreign Affairs, who would act as the WRB's representative. When Olsen chose Wallenberg for the job, he probably also recruited him to join the OSS (see Feature, opposite), which could explain his arrest by the Soviet authorities and his execution in Moscow in July 1947, during one of Stalin's many vengeful killing sprees.

Diplomatic immunity

Wallenberg arrived in Budapest in July 1944 when the deportations were at their height and only an estimated 250,000 Jews remained in the whole of Hungary. He immediately began to issue Swedish passports to as many of the survivors as he could find, thus preventing their deportations, though sometimes he also had to bribe German and Hungarian officials to ensure their freedom. Using WRB funds, Wallenberg rented over 30 buildings in Budapest, declaring them to be protected by diplomatic immunity, in which he sheltered 10,000 refugees. At its height Wallenberg's network employed 350 agents, including diplomats from other neutral countries and SOE operatives.

FEATURE | **Was Wallenberg an OSS spy?**

Wallenberg's fate after the war remains something of a mystery, but it is one on which some light has now been shed. In 1996, the Central Intelligence Agency, the successor to the wartime Office of Strategic Services, released thousands of classified documents under the 50-year rule. These revealed that when Wallenberg was conducting his humanitarian work in Hungary, he was also liaising with the OSS and the Hungarian opposition and resistance movements. It seems likely that American Intelligence had recruited Wallenberg before he had been appointed to represent the WRB in Hungary. Hence he would have had the dual mission of saving Hungary's Jews and destabilizing its pro-Nazi government. His arrest, detention, and probable execution by the Soviet authorities, however, do not confirm that Wallenberg was an American spy—other East European humanitarians with no espionage connections, such as Irena Sendler (pp. 208–211), were also persecuted after the war.

One of his most daring rescues was when he delayed the departure of a train taking Jews to Auschwitz-Birkenau. According to his driver's testimony, Wallenberg climbed on to the roof of the train, oblivious to the guards' orders and warning shots, and handed out Swedish passports to the passengers. Once he exhausted his supply of passports, he led several dozen Jews off the train to a waiting line of cars flying Swedish flags. Although his actions made him a target for the SS, he managed to survive the German occupation, and even persuaded the German commander to spare the 70,000 Jews left in the Budapest Ghetto.

ABOVE:
As soon as the Germans had taken over, they began the systematic destruction of Hungary's ancient Jewish community.

Further Reading

There are many excellent general reference works available in printed form or online covering the many of the entries featured in this book. Still one of the most authoritative is the *Encyclopædia Britannica*, available for free at most large public and school libraries, and online at *britannica.com* as a subscription service. Another reference source that is used by authors and journalists is the ubiquitous Wikipedia (en.wikipedia.org). The content of Wikipedia, however, is user-generated, and is not independently verified. As a result there are inaccurate or biased articles included in the database (articles identified as having problems or a particular bias are often flagged by the site, but the site itself will not edit or delete articles unless they are proved to be bogus or libelous). Nevertheless, Wikipedia and its associated sites provide a good starting point to find basic information and references on a wide range of topics.

Judith Baumel-Schwartz, *Never Look Back: The Jewish Refugee Children in Great Britain, 1938–1945* (West Lafayette, Indiana, 2012)

James Bentley, *Martin Niemoeller* (New York, 1984)

Michael Berenbaum and Abraham Peck, *The Holocaust and History: The Known, the Unknown, the Disputed, and the Reexamined* (Bloomington, Indiana, 1998)

Marcus Binney, *The Women Who Lived for Danger: The Women Agents of SOE in the Second World War* (London, 2002)

Rupert Butler, *Stalin's Secret Police: A History of the Cheka, Ogpu, Nkvd, Smersh and KGB: 1917–1991* (London, 2015)

Matthew Cobb, *The Resistance: The French Fight against the Nazis* (New York, 2009)

John W. Dower, *Embracing Defeat: Japan in the Wake of World War II* (New York, 1999)

Olga Drucker, *Kindertransport* (New York, 1998)

Beryl Escott, *Heroines of SOE: Britain's Secret Women in France* (London Press, 2012).

Peter FitzSimons, *Nancy Wake: A Biography of Our Greatest War Heroine* (Pymble, New South Wales, 2002)

Robert Gildea, *Fighters in the Shadows: A New History of the French Resistance* (London, 2015)

Max Hastings, *The Secret War: Spies, Codes and Guerrillas 1939–1945* (London, 2015)

Peter Hoffmann, *German Resistance to Hitler* (Cambridge, Massachusetts, 1988)

Ian Hogg, *German Secret Weapons of World War II: The Missiles, Rockets, Weapons and New Technology of the Third Reich* (Barnsley, South Yorkshire, 2015)

Dick Horton, *Ring of Fire: Australian Guerilla Operations Against the Japanese in World War II* (London, 1983)

Julian Jackson, *France: The dark years, 1940–1944* (Oxford, 2001)

Julian Jackson, *The Fall of France: The Nazi Invasion of 1940* (Oxford, 2003)

Sophie Jackson, *Churchill's White Rabbit: The True Story of a Real-life James Bond* (London, 2012)

Eric T. Jennings, *Free French Africa in World War II: The African Resistance* (Cambridge, 2015)

Christer Jorgensen, *Hitler's Espionage Machine: German Intelligence Agencies and Operations During World War II* (Staplehurst, Kent, 2004)

Patrick Marnham, *The Death of Jean Moulin: Biography of a Ghost* (New York, 2001)

Charles Marsh, *Strange Glory: A Life of Dietrich Bonhoeffer* (New York, 2014)

Frank McDonough, *Sophie Scholl: The Real Story of the Woman Who Defied Hitler* (London, 2009)

Frank McDonough, *The Gestapo: The Myth and Reality of Hitler's Secret Police* (London, 2015)

Sinclair McKay, *The Secret Life of Bletchley Park: The History of the Wartime Codebreaking Centre by the Men and Women Who Were There* (London, 2011)

Mordecai Paldiel, *Saving the Jews: Men and Women who Defied the Final Solution* (Lanham, Maryland, 2011)

Richard Rhodes, *The Making of the Atomic Bomb* (New York, 1986)

Dean G. Stroud, *Preaching in Hitler's Shadow: Sermons of Resistance in the Third Reich* (Grand Rapids, Michigan, 2013)

Leopold Trepper and H. Weaver, *The Great Game: Memoirs of the Spy Hitler Couldn't Silence* (New York, 1977)

Nancy Wake, *Autobiography of the Woman the Gestapo Called the White Mouse* (Melbourne, Victoria, 1985)

Stephen Walker, *Hide & Seek: The Irish Priest In The Vatican Who Defied The Nazi Command* (London, 2011)

Robert Whymant (2006) *Stalin's Spy: Richard Sorge and the Tokyo Espionage Ring* (New York, 2006)

Reggie L. Williams, *Bonhoeffer's Black Jesus: Harlem Renaissance Theology and an Ethic of Resistance* (Waco, Texas, 2014)

Image credits

9: © Bundesarchiv, Bild 183-1987-0703-507 | CC-BY-SA 3.0
16: © J. A. Hamption | Stringer
17: © Dr. Sahay | Creative Commons
21: © Bundesarchiv, Bild 101I-641-4548-24 | Wanderer, W. |
     CC-BY-SA 3.0
22: © Bundesarchiv, Bild 101I-662-6660-27A | Ketelhohn
     [Kettelhohn] | CC-BY-SA 3.0
26: © Franck Cabrol | Creative Commons
32: © Heritage Images | Contributor
33: © Evening Standard | Stringer
34: © Times Life Pictures | Contributor
40: © Keystone | Stringer
42 top: © Creative Commons
48: © Bundesarchiv, Bild 101I-228-0326-34A | Dey | CC-BY-SA 3.0
51: © Archive Photos | Stringer
54: © Apic | Contributor
55: © Hanedoes | Creative Commons
58: © Apic | Contributor
60: © Bundesarchiv, Bild 146-1989-107-24 | Koll | CC-BY-SA 3.0
63: © Efarestv | Creative Commons
68: © Bundesarchiv, Bild 183-J27289 | Koll | CC-BY-SA 3.0
69: © Bundesarchiv, Bild 152-11-12 | CC-BY-SA 3.0
70: © Keystone | Stringer
76: © UK National Archives
79: © Bundesarchiv, Bild 183-1985-0417-15 | CC-BY-SA 3.0
87: © Galerie Bilderwelt | Contributor
92: © Time & Life Pictures | Contributor
94: © Bundesarchiv, Bild 183-1985-1003-020 | CC-BY-SA 3.0
95: © Bundesarchiv, B 145 Bild-P046279 | Weinrother, Carl |
     CC-BY-SA 3.0
96: © Bundesarchiv, Bild 119-11-19-12 | CC-BY-SA 3.0
100: © Bundesarchiv, Bild 146-1969-118-88 | CC-BY-SA 3.0
101: © Bundesarchiv, Bild 183-H04436 | CC-BY-SA 3.0
102: © Getty Images
103: © Bundesarchiv, Bild 183-R80329 | CC-BY-SA 3.0
107: © Bundesarchiv, Bild 102-14468 | Georg Pahl | CC-BY-SA 3.0
108: © Bundesarchiv, Bild 101I-017-1065-44A | Becker |
     CC-BY-SA 3.0
112: © Bundesarchiv, Bild 183-R97512 | CC-BY-SA 3.0
113: © Bundesarchiv, Bild 183-1983-0825-303 | CC-BY-SA 3.0
116: © Rachel Zylberberg | Creative Commons
120: © Bundesarchiv, Bild 146-1980-033-04 | CC-BY-SA 3.0
121: © Bundesarchiv, Bild 102-13902 | CC-BY-SA 3.0
122: © Bundesarchiv, Bild 146-1990-044-13 | CC-BY-SA 3.0
123: © Bundesarchiv, Bild 136-B3516 | Tellgmann, Gustav |
     CC-BY-SA
124: © Bundesarchiv, Bild 146-1987-074-16 | CC-BY-SA 3.0
125: © Bundesarchiv, Bild 183-R0211-316 | CC-BY-SA 3.0
130: © Henri Moreau | Creative Commons
131: © Notabene | Creative Commons
132: © Keystone-France | Contributor
133: © Bundesarchiv, Bild 146-1983-077-14A | Licht | CC-BY-SA 3.0
135 top: © Creative Commons

135 bottom: © Keystone-France | Contributor
136: © Bundesarchiv, Bild 146-1979-013-43 | CC-BY-SA 3.0
139: © Bundesarchiv, Bild 183-H15527 | CC-BY-SA 3.0
140: © Apic | Contributor
141 top: © PhotoQuest | Contributor
143: © Bundesarchiv, Bild 183-H25217 | CC-BY-SA 3.0
144: © Gustav Albers | Creative Commons
145: © Dietmar Rabich, rabich.de | Creative Commons
146: © Bundesarchiv, Bild 183-R24391 |
     Unknownwikidata:Q4233718 | CC-BY-SA 3.0
147: © Djampa | Creative Commons
151: © Flexicon | Creative Commons
152: © Nationaal Archief | Creative Commons
153: © Bundesarchiv, Bild 102-15234 | CC-BY-SA 3.0
158: © Keystone | Stringer
159: © Bundesarchiv, Bild 101I-129-0480-25 | Boesig, Heinz |
     CC-BY-SA
162: © Ullstein Bild | Contributor
163: © Ullstein Bild | Contributor
168: © Ullstein Bild | Contributor
169: © Ullstein Bild | Contributor
171: © Bundesarchiv, Bild 146-1972-025-10 | CC-BY-SA 3.0
172: © Ullstein Bild | Contributor
173: © Bundesarchiv, Bild 151-43-22A | CC-BY-SA 3.0
176: © Popperfoto | Contributor
178: © Keystone | Staff
179 bottom: © Satmi9 | Creative Commons
183: © Creative Commons
184: © Fred Stein Archive | Contributor
185: © Bundesarchiv, Bild 102-14468 | Georg Pahl | CC-BY-SA 3.0
187: © Apic | Contributor
188: © Nationaal Archief | Creative Commons
189 both: © Anne Frank Fonds Basel | Contributor
190: © Massimo Catarinella | Creative Commons
191: © CBS Photo Archive | Contributor
196: © Moliere | Creative Commons
197: © Hans Wild | Contributor
198: © PHAS | Contributor
204: © Keystone | Stringer
205: © Jennifer Boyer | Creative Commons
209: © Bundesarchiv, Bild 101I-134-0791-29A | Knobloch, Ludwig |
     CC-BY-SA 3.0
214: © Getty Images
216: © Bundesarchiv, Bild 101I-680-8283A-12A | Faupel |
     CC-BY-SA 3.0
217: © Bundesarchiv, Bild 183-74237-004 | CC-BY-SA 3.0

Illustrations by Tony Seddon.

All other images are in the public domain.